APR 2009

LI

looking for hickories

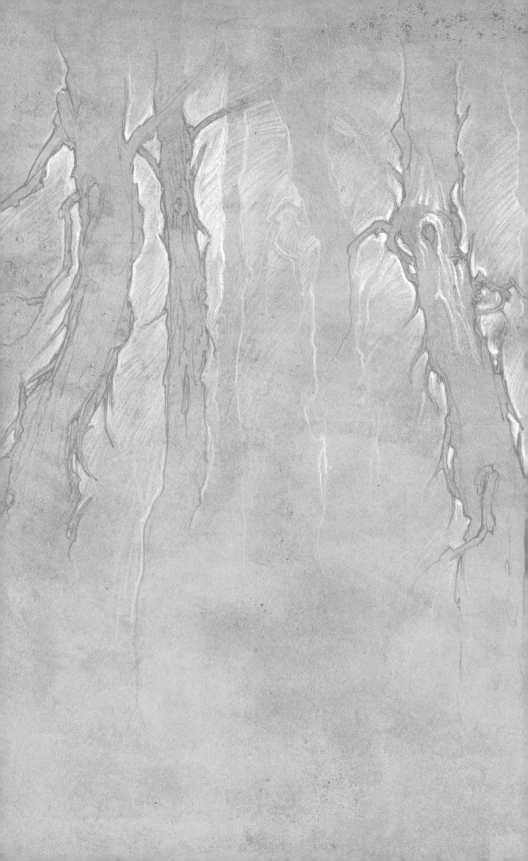

looking for hickories

THE FORGOTTEN
WILDNESS OF THE
RURAL MIDWEST

TOM SPRINGER

The University of Michigan Press
Ann Arbor

Copyright © by Tom Springer 2008
All rights reserved
Published in the United States of America by
The University of Michigan Press
Manufactured in the United States of America
⊗ Printed on acid-free paper

2011   2010   2009   2008   4   3   2   1

A CIP catalog record for this book is available from the British Library.

Library of Congress Cataloging-in-Publication Data

Springer, Tom, 1959–
     Looking for hickories : the forgotten wildness of the rural
Midwest / Tom Springer.
          p.   cm.
     ISBN-13: 978-0-472-07023-7 (cloth : alk. paper)
     ISBN-10: 0-472-07023-1 (cloth : alk. paper)
     ISBN-13: 978-0-472-05023-9 (pbk. : alk. paper)
     ISBN-10: 0-472-05023-0 (pbk. : alk. paper)
     1. Natural history—Middle West—Anecdotes.   2. Wilderness areas—
Middle West—Anecdotes.   3. Springer, Tom, 1959–   I. Title.

QH104.5.M47S67   2008
508.78—dc22   2007031013

ILLUSTRATIONS ARE BY *Ladislav Hanka*.

ACKNOWLEDGMENTS

I have been blessed by many teachers, friends, and family members who have enabled me to pursue this work. The first is my mother, Dolores Springer, an avid reader who instilled in me, and all her children, an abiding love for the printed page. Those summer afternoons when she read us *Wizard of Oz* books while the Sears fan droned on the bedroom floor of our cinder block home in Melbourne, Florida, are among my happiest memories.

As for classroom teachers, I owe much to Raelyn Joyce, a now retired English professor at Kalamazoo Valley Community College. At a time when I was studying for a two-year degree in furnace repair, she encouraged me to be something I'd never known I could be: a writer.

Through internships, jobs, and military service, I've been guided by great bosses and writing mentors such as Blaine Lam, Lew Tysman, Bob Hencey, Karen Whalen, Carl Stoddard, Danny Vander Myde, and Dawn Dancer.

During graduate school at Michigan State University's School of Journalism, it was Professor Howard Bossen who first suggested that I write essays of this sort. Later it was the expert instruction of MSU professors Laura Julier, Eric Freedman, and Jim Detjen that allowed me to follow this new direction. (Jim Detjen also showed me that it's OK to take off your shoes at work.)

Once you write essays, it's helpful if a kindly editor will buy them. My first such editor was Dennis Knickerbocker, the former editor of *Michigan Out-of-Doors*. Another is Kerry Temple of *Notre Dame* magazine, who astounded me by running "Trees Can Lead You Home" in his fine publication.

During my foray into public radio, my essay writing benefited greatly from generous professionals who tried to teach me the art, and technology, of audio storytelling. From the Great Lakes Radio Consortium, I am thankful to David Hammond, Mark Brush, and Dale Willman. From Michigan Radio, Erin Toner and Sarah Hulett showed me more encouragement and support than a beginner deserves. If they wonder why my radio work tailed off, I hope this book will serve as a plausible excuse.

Three other people figured significantly in the production of this book. The first is my friend, coworker, and fellow writer Mike Van-Buren. There's no need for Mike to read this book since during our lunchtime workouts he's heard all of these essays delivered in oral form.

Mary Erwin, my editor at the University of Michigan Press, is an exceedingly patient and encouraging woman. She saw promise in a manuscript that needed a total rewrite and then gave me nearly a year to rest and heal before I got back to the task. Thank-you, thank-you.

Ladislav Hanka, whose mystically beautiful illustrations grace these pages, has been a most welcome surprise. Wish I'd met him much sooner. Lad's a principled fellow, a citizen of the world who nonetheless loves all things wild and native. His art speaks for itself, as does his homemade sassafras brandy.

Have I missed anyone? Well, there is God, and his holy communion of angels and saints, without whose constant intercession I'd be lost, broken, and unredeemed. I hope to profit from their care long after this book has been recycled into junk mail or sold for twenty-five cents at a library book sale.

Finally, and primarily, there is my wife Nancy. She doesn't share my love of writing. But she does share something much more important and lasting, which is our marriage, family, and life together. And that's the best happy ending of all.

CONTENTS

FORGOTTEN WATERS

WINTER, DEATH, AND OTHER COUNTRY PLEASURES

ROOTS, NUTS, AND
BRANCHES

LOOKING FOR HICKORIES

Rediscovering the Virtues of an American Icon

In my hometown of Three Rivers, Michigan, the school superintendent used to publish a newsletter called the *Hickory Stick*. It carried articles about field trips and science fairs, and the words *Hickory Stick* were written in letters that resembled Lincoln Logs.

During the mid-1980s, the newsletter's name was changed to the *Educator*. While the newer name sounds blandly institutional, it was an understandable concession to modern thinking. In American tradition, the hickory stick has long been associated with harsh discipline. Teachers once kept a hickory switch handy to whack the hands and backsides of errant pupils.

The hickory, of course, asked for none of this. Since we've put school-approved corporal punishment "behind" us, there's no need to further malign the tree's character. Our native hickory, from its versatile wood to its fiery gold autumn foliage, deserves a renewed sense of respect and affection. As for the rare flavor of hickory nuts—well, more on that momentarily.

In Michigan, there wouldn't even be hickories if the state line were located a few hundred miles north. Hickories grow across much of the United States and Mexico but reach the northern limits of their range in southern Michigan. The Lower Peninsula is home to four species: pignut, shagbark, shellbark, and bitternut.

Wherever it's found, the hickory is rugged through and through. Most prefer sandy or gravelly soil, the same dry terrain favored by black oak and black cherry. Even the hickory's oval leaves are tough and leathery. When crumbled, they emit a spicy, peppery smell—no subtle fragrance here.

The bark is gray and smooth on saplings but forms loose strips and rough, interlacing ridges on mature trees. The shagbark hickory, as its name suggests, looks especially rustic and unkempt. Its bark curls away from the trunk in long strips that "look like they were left in the rain too long" in the words of Michigan naturalist John Eastman.

Given its robust form and function, it's no wonder the hickory was once an American icon. And no one has described its mythic status better than the botanist and wordsmith Donald Culross Peattie.

> To everyone with a feeling for things American, and for American history, the shagbark [hickory] seems like a symbol of the pioneer age, with its hard sinewy limbs and rude, shaggy coat, like the pioneer himself in fringed deerskin hunting shirt. And the roaring heat of its fire, the tang of its nuts—that wild manna that every autumn it once cast lavishly before the feet—stand for the days of forest abundance.

As for the hickory's sinewy mettle, I once encountered it while I was clearing brush and stumbled backward into a two-inch-diameter sapling. The little tree shuddered with an audible hum. When I whacked it again, this time with my open palm, its trunk vibrated like an oversized tuning fork. It's this resiliency that makes hickory such a popular choice for shovel, ax, and sledgehammer handles.

On a fall day a few years ago, my brother and I cut down a dead hickory in our woods along the Portage River in St. Joseph County. It was a golden November afternoon, unseasonably warm, and before long our boots were powdered with fragrant sawdust. This same aroma brings a sweet, tang to hickory-smoked meats and barbecue sauce. (Wood chips from the bitternut hickory—whose nuts are nearly inedible—are said to impart the best flavor.)

As I pushed a loaded wheelbarrow down the path to our pickup truck, I saw a few stray chunks of hickory firewood from last year's cutting. They had already turned soft and soggy. Contrary as it may seem, the wood from this famously rugged tree rots quickly once in contact with soil, so we left these pieces for the ants and termites to

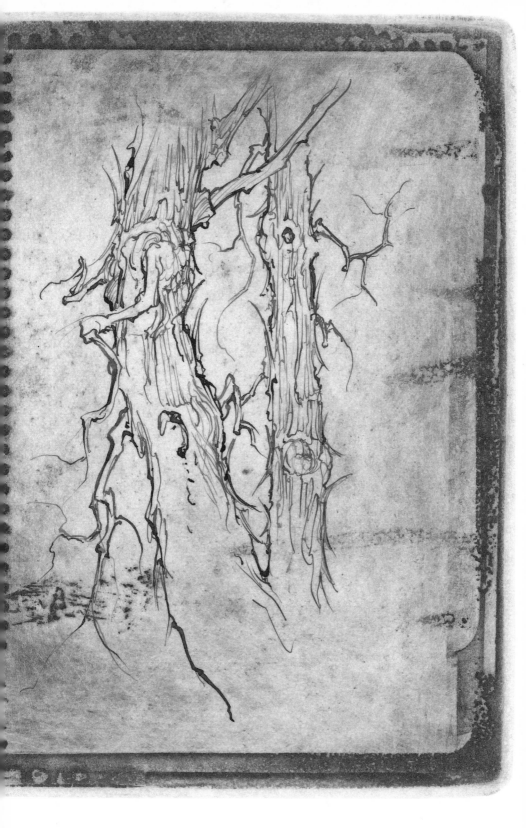

enjoy. You wouldn't want to use hickory for a fence or mailbox post. Osage orange would be the thing for that.

The tree we cut was about ten inches in diameter, and with a five-pound maul we easily split the lengths into halves and quarters for use in a fireplace. And for that hickory is hard to beat. Because the wood is so dense, a cord of dry hickory gives off as much heat as a ton of coal or two hundred gallons of number 2 fuel oil.

It would be a mistake, however, to assume that the only place for hickory lumber is in a tool shed or woodpile. Increasingly, as other hardwoods become more expensive, hickory is being used for furniture and kitchen cabinets. It has a close grain, a creamy beige hue, and a smattering of small, wavy knots that woodworkers call "bird peck." After seeing hickory consigned to ax handle status for so many years, it's nice to see the wood finely milled and polished, the way oak or cherry cabinets usually are.

Now, with regard to the nuts, we could still learn much from those spirited pioneer schoolkids who were reared, so to speak, in the days when virgin groves of hickories once stood near most midwestern farms and villages. What boys and girls once collected by the bushel for their autumn "nut crack" parties has now become a culinary rarity.

By coincidence, about a week after my brother and I cut up the hickory for firewood, I received a gourmet food catalog in the mail. Along with designer jams, preserves, and dried fruit, the catalog offered wild hickory nuts—$6.95 for a four-ounce package. The price seemed outlandish, so I decided to harvest my own from beneath a fifty-foot tree that grows near our driveway.

That night, after three and a half hours of cracking and picking, I managed to glean a *single cup* of hickory nut meats. At that pace, I'd have to sell my nuts at about seventeen dollars per four-ounce package just to earn the minimum wage. Nonetheless, it was a peaceful way to pass an evening. I cracked and picked with an old plastic bowl on my lap while the film *Forrest Gump* played on television.

About 20 percent of the nuts had small holes the size of a pinhead. Inside these, there was usually a squirmy, white intruder. To paraphrase Forrest Gump, "Life is like a bowl of hickory nuts. You never know when you'll run into a big, fat worm."

The next night we were warmed inside and out by the hickory's bounty. We ate hickory nut cookies fresh from the oven (made from a recipe in the gourmet food catalog, thank-you) while an armload of hickory logs flared in the fireplace. The only thing better, it seems, would be a slice of fresh hickory nut pie. And that's ample enticement to pick another batch of nuts next year.

For all its charms, the hickory is in dire need of a marketing campaign. When I told friends and coworkers about the tasty cookies (alas, there were none left to share), they were surprised to hear that hickory nuts were so readily available. The gourmet food catalog—perhaps hoping to justify its high prices—described hickories as "living antiques that are very difficult to find."

The truth is hickories are quite common across the Midwest. As with many native species, the tree goes unnoticed and unloved by an urbanized population. Each year tons of hickory nuts fall to the ground unheeded, like so many uncounted blessings. Or at least unheeded by humans. The nuts are an important food for turkeys, wood ducks, chipmunks, squirrels, and whatever those little white worms are.

Does a hickory grow in your yard? If so, consider yourself lucky. It's no doubt a living monument to the vanished woods that once occupied your property. The hickory's long taproot makes it difficult to transplant, so it's unlikely that a landscaper placed it there. Of course, if you're a patient person you can buy hickory saplings from a specialty nursery. You'll just need to wait twenty years for your tree to produce any nuts.

But think ahead to a fall evening when the grandkids stop by for their first plate of hickory nut cookies. Unaware of the hickory's tough love persona, maybe they'll someday find room for a tree in their yard—or at least in their heart.

FORGOTTEN FOSSILS FROM
A LOCAL WORLD

I knew for certain it was the petrified fang of a saber-toothed tiger. My friend Jody and I had just plucked it from the black muck of a Florida creek bed. First the saber tooth, then in frantic profusion a brontosaurus bone and what was no doubt a velociraptor vertebra. We found so many so quickly it was intoxicating—like a waking dream of buried treasure.

In the way of most natural discoveries, the moment was magic and unexpected. Jody told me at school about the fossil bed, and we pedaled to the creek after baseball practice. We parked our bikes at the small bridge, its pavement warm, its blackened timbers sweet with the scent of sun-baked creosote. Then down through the head-high swamp grass, splashing into the creek shallows, cloaked in cool tendrils of early evening air from the nearby marsh.

Within seconds, though just a few feet from the road, we were a world away from the dusty logic of adults and classrooms. The alchemy of childhood turned each shell and hunk of porous stone into a rare and wonderful fossil. Suddenly we were more than just nine-year-old suburban kids trapped in a monoscape of puny palm trees and cinder block houses. We were boy gods, present at the exhuming of creation. I had never felt such a sense of wild discovery.

What became of these artifacts, whatever they were, I don't recall. But that feeling, of kneeling at dusk with wet sneakers and the world's mysteries revealed at my feet, is a touchstone memory of childhood.

As adults, it's a shame that we can no longer find dinosaur bones in a muddy stream by the margins of a subdivision. Or see—really see—Spanish galleons in the cumulus clouds of a Cape Canaveral sky. If you're like me, your inner child had to move out and get a day job some time ago. And with its departure went our ability to find excitement in the everyday wonders around us.

It is, alas, a common spiritual and civic disorder. In an urbanized world, we tend to assume that any worthwhile encounter with nature must take place elsewhere. Yearning for Yellowstone, we overlook the fossils in our own backyard (not to mention the red-tailed hawk in the little cattail marsh down the street). For adults, and especially for children, this is a sad and deeply unhealthy situation.

It would take a team of social scientists to explain the long history of our growing disconnect from the natural world. But one obvious factor is the way we've obliterated the native landscapes that give each region its distinct character. Don't expect, for instance, to find big bluestem grass or white oak trees outside a midwestern strip mall. From coast to coast, we've created a United States of Generica, replete with mass-produced landscapes that look like everywhere else—and nowhere in particular.

For a people so proud of their diversity, this is a curious development. In other respects, America is a land of increasingly diffuse values, opinions, tastes, and interests. On this much, however, we seem to agree: any respectable building, public or private, shall be ringed by islands of bark chips or bogus lava rock spread over black plastic. Further, these grounds shall be carpeted with pampered turf grass and dotted with obligatory clumps of nonnative burning bush and Japanese maple. And that's about it. As with any franchise, the standard plan varies little. In fact, that's the whole idea.

Yet, for all we spend to maintain them, our man-made landscapes are strangely devoid of people. When's the last time you saw anyone—aside from a lawn care crew—actually set foot on the moats of green space that surround most malls and office parks? These places might as well be the dead zone that surrounds Chernobyl.

As our daily encounters with the natural world dwindle, it's no wonder that we seek exotic relief from the tyranny of deodorant and panty hose. Again, for grown-ups who lead busy, compartmentalized lives, it's easy to look for these encounters elsewhere. Today's eco-tourism industry allows the masses to pursue what were once the adventures of a maverick few: hunting bears and caribou in Alaska, white-water rafting through the Grand Canyon, deep-sea fishing off the coast of Belize.

It's all good fun, but here's the drawback: It's hard to appreciate local wildness after feasting on the splendor of five-star wilderness. As a backpacker and fisherman, I know I've been spoiled by the trout streams and virgin hemlock forests of Michigan's Upper Peninsula. Between vacations, it's easy to stash away my sense of adventure with the hip waders and muddy hiking boots. There's some pretty scenery near my rural home, but out here in cornfield country I've never expected any wild epiphanies.

But it was a coyote—and a dead one at that—that helped me to see things differently.

I found him lying alongside the quiet road where I'd been jogging on a Saturday morning in June. He was a small male, about twenty-five pounds. His charcoal-colored coat was tinged with auburn. For several years, I'd heard that coyotes were in the area, but this was my first piece of evidence. With a find like this, there was only one thing to do: track down my nephew Nick, who, like most kids, has a healthy fascination with all things dead.

Half an hour later, as Nick nudged the coyote with a stick, something stirred inside me. Suddenly this was more than a carcass. He was a totem of something wild and forgotten, a relic of an untamed past I thought was gone forever. It made me think anew about the long-settled landscape I call home. If this could live here, what else might?

The feeling passed, although I couldn't forget the coyotes. My brother and I heard them howling one night out beyond the marsh, harmonizing with the whistle of a freight train. Too bad Nick was already in bed.

Then, six months later, the wild spirit returned for another visit, albeit in a different form. On a Sunday in January, out of boredom, I suggested to my wife that we go cross-country skiing near our home. I say boredom because if there's a hill higher than a pitcher's mound within miles of our house I've never seen it. In my corner of south-ern Michigan, you ski for exercise not excitement.

Still, there was good snow and a bright sky as we set out across a cornfield. We followed a hedgerow, which led to a narrow belt of woods. There, the little creek I had always dismissed as a drainage ditch was frozen over—a rare occurrence.

Tentatively at first, we eased onto the tiny waterway. And then, somehow, it was as if we'd stepped through a secret window into the wilderness. We rushed with abandon along a clear ribbon of ice. Alongside us rose wind-sculpted banks of snow, carved smooth as white marble. Overhead a vault of trees and sky and beneath us the whoosh of skis on ice and the pock-pock of poles as we strained for more speed and power.

And again that childhood sense of transformation. The woods along the stream was a thicket of scrubby oaks and bittersweet vines that you could barely walk through. But on the frozen stream a few feet away movement was as effortless as thought. When I try to describe the feeling now, it is boyhood images that come to mind. I felt like Hans Brinker, streaking on silver skates along the canals of Amsterdam. I felt like a five year old who has just been told, and now believes, that his grandpa's '65 Ford sedan can fly.

After that episode, I wised up a bit. Even out here in cornfield country I suspected there might be more pockets of natural magic. I began to look consciously, but of course I did not find them. "Nature," as Lao-tzu once said, "is not human-hearted."

A few months later, I drove to a nearby stretch of the St. Joseph River. I was with Nick again, whose parents had gone to Romania to adopt his new little sister. An afternoon on the river seemed like a good remedy for a lonely and anxious kid. We fished awhile, but after catching only a few small bass we decided to call it quits. Then, walking back to the car, something caught my eye.

It was a pendulous globe of green, hanging from its stem like a miniature banana. The tree's huge, oblong leaves made it seem like a refugee from a Brazilian jungle. There was no mistaking this find. It was the fruit that had been the manna of Indians, explorers, and hungry settlers: the wild pawpaw. The pawpaw's taste is sweet and pungent, a custardy blend of strawberry and banana. You can't buy them in stores, because pawpaws are not grown commercially. Pawpaws grow in thickets, and they especially thrive in the black, rich soil of a floodplain forest.

A few moments later, Nick spotted his own dangling pawpaw. And that's when another window opened on the universe. Above that pawpaw was a whole cluster, and behind that was another tree, and beyond that was a remarkable sight. Along both sides of the road, camouflaged by a stand of silver maples, stood one of the biggest pawpaw patches I had ever seen. I'd driven this road dozens of times but never noticed.

We talked about pawpaws all the way home and for several days after that. This was our find. After the first hard frost, when the pawpaws were speckled black and properly ripened, we'd return for the harvest.

The human mind is a tireless creature, forever at work to find useful solutions and helpful connections on our behalf. And so it was that the afternoon's events led me to discover yet another hidden treasure.

A few days later, for the first time in thirty years, I remembered the dinosaur bones that I'd unearthed from the untamed margins of a Melbourne, Florida, subdivision. As memories do, it just popped into my head while I was supposed to be doing something else. But to have this memory restored was a rare blessing. It affirmed that what I'd loved and valued as a child had never left; it had merely matured and taken new form. Once again I'd found wonder in a local place that at first glance seemed unremarkable.

For some reason, Nick and I never made it back to the riverbank that fall. I got busy with work and house renovation projects, and Nick was caught up with school and the arrival of a new kid sister. But maybe the moment we had together is what mattered most. I want to believe that the pawpaws have become more than a basket of fruit to gather on a golden October morning. They have, I hope, become a touchstone of wildness—a rare fossil embedded in a young boy's memory of home.

TREES CAN LEAD YOU HOME

There was a recent story in a Detroit newspaper about the landscaping "problem" that faces people who build enormous homes in midwestern suburbs. As the article explained, most subdivisions are built on farmland without many shade trees to begin with. To make matters worse, a standard eight-foot sapling looks like a leafy broomstick when planted next to a five-thousand-square-foot, faux colonial mansion.

The obvious solution—at least for moneyed homeowners—is to plant bigger trees, and landscapers and nursery owners are happy to oblige. By using a truck-mounted hydraulic spade, a landscaping crew can transplant a mature tree up to forty feet tall. Although trees this size can easily cost five thousand dollars apiece, the nursery owners quoted in the article said they were struggling to meet the demand. To paraphrase F. Scott Fitzgerald, the rich are different from you and me—they don't have to wait for their trees to grow.

Our farmhouse is surrounded on all sides by sun-scorched fields of corn, potatoes, and watermelons. And we, too, would like some more shade around the property. Yet there's a wheezy pump in the basement that needs fixing, and our monthly heating bill in winter often exceeds our mortgage payment. We know where our money's going for the next few years, and it won't be to line a landscaper's pocket.

But for anyone who's unable or unwilling to spend six figures on nursery-grown shade trees, there's a simple, low-cost alternative:

you can grow your own from scratch. You'll be in good company if you do, since that's how the Almighty raised up the cedars of Lebanon and the coastal redwoods of California. In other words, from acorns, nuts, pinecones, and the seedlings that whirl down from sugar maples like squadrons of little green helicopters.

There's a contrary logic to the do-it-yourself approach that's perversely appealing. If you can't afford to have the biggest trees, then why not have the smallest? And instead of trying to outspend your neighbor why not grow trees for next to nothing with seeds collected from wild, and thereby free, sources?

My career in microforestry began on a bright October day as my wife and I walked the dog down our country road. During one of the dog's endless pit stops, I gathered a half-dozen hickory nuts and dropped them in the pocket of my army field jacket. The nuts were forgotten once we returned home, and the coat hung undisturbed in the closet until spring. After being rediscovered in March, the nuts were planted in one-quart milk cartons, filled with garden soil, and placed on a sunny windowsill

In this case, my habitual procrastination turned out to be provident. To become fertile, most wild seeds require a season of dormancy, and the dark, cool closet was an ideal place for hibernation. By spring, the nuts were rested and ready. By late May, four of the six had thrust a toothpick-sized shoot toward the heavens. It was an alleluia moment—a simple miracle wrought from the elemental ingredients of water, soil, and sunlight.

This year, my indoor forest has been enlarged. It now occupies a three-foot shelf beneath two east-facing windows in an unheated storeroom. There, in little cardboard containers, I planted seeds from hickories, burr oaks, white oaks, honey locusts, and sycamores. Their stock was chosen carefully from strong, well-limbed trees whose vigor bespeaks good parentage. After two years, the seedlings can be replanted outside, or given to like-minded friends who appreciate things native and free.

Raising trees from scratch is an inexpensive hobby, and filling cartons with soil and seed is a relaxing way to pass an evening. As hobbies go, microforestry doesn't require special equipment, clothing, instruction, or user fees. But there's a catch. In modern America, such an anticonsumptive pastime may mark you as a suspicious character.

On a Sunday afternoon, I went to gather acorns from an ancient burr oak along U.S. 131, a busy four-lane highway in Southwest Michigan. This magnificent tree has a craggy crown that evokes the gnarled wisdom and splendor of an Old Testament prophet. Given its size, the tree must have borne witness to Indian hunting parties, pioneer wagons, and the boundless flocks of passenger pigeons that once darkened the midwestern sky. I was so happily absorbed by these thoughts that I never saw the bright blue sedan pull up.

"Excuse me sir, can I ask what you're doing?" the state trooper asked.

"Well, uh, I'm gathering acorns," I said. "I'm going to plant them and grow my own trees."

He looked at me with a mixture of bemusement and pity. Somewhat flustered, I rambled on about the beautiful burr oak, and how saving its acorns would allow me to propagate its progeny.

"You know," he said, looking past my shoulder as cars and trucks zipped by, "I drive by that tree every day, but I guess I'm just too busy to notice that kind of thing." He told me to be careful around traffic, which probably seemed like a necessary precaution when you're dealing with a middle-aged man who gets excited about acorns.

The contraband acorns are safe at home now, tucked in a bed of black potting soil. When they become seedlings, they'll join the 150 larger trees that have been transplanted to build a windbreak around our acreage. These saplings were collected from fields, forests, backyards and vacant suburban lots that were about to be scraped clean by bulldozers. Any gaps that appear in the windbreak will be filled with seedlings from the windowsill greenhouse. It's the latest tactic in a small-scale reforestation campaign that began the first autumn after we bought our house.

Yet, if you're a tiny tree, this is where the story turns dramatic or, as is often the case, traumatic. Getting seeds to sprout in a windowsill sanctuary is a hobby. Helping naked, defenseless seedlings survive in a wild environment is more of a vocation. And, like any true vocation, it will redirect your life in ways you never expected.

During the first spring in our new home, I bought a batch of seedlings from the county conservation district—tulip poplar, white oak, red oak, and butternut. It seemed so easy then. Dig a hole every fifteen feet, plop in a seedling, add some water, and wait.

Of the one hundred seedlings I planted that April, only five were alive by the next spring. After several of the more robust seedlings leafed out in May, a late frost turned their tender growth into wilted blobs of chlorophyll. Then came a month-long summer drought that claimed dozens more seedlings while we were away on vacation. In October, a band of rambunctious deer scraped their antlers on the largest saplings until the bark hung in ragged tatters. In winter, when all seemed peaceful beneath a white robe of snow, rabbits and field mice killed even more trees by gnawing off the bark around the trunk as clean as if you'd whittled it bare with a jackknife.

I have a bookshelf full of tree guides and am always bugging land-scapers and nurserymen for tips on tree care. Yet the experts tend to speak in generalities that are often less than helpful. Each individual tree follows its own interpretations of natural law, and it's our job to figure out what makes them act and adapt as they do.

But this much is certain: Any tree that survives until maturity in the wild is a statistical oddity. No wonder the ancient druids considered trees divine. The energy, luck, and grace required for a bare acorn to become a thick-trunked oak in the face of animal predation, insects, disease, lightning, and drought borders on the miraculous. If you want proof, go plant a hundred seedlings on the weedy, dusty margins of a Michigan cornfield.

Beyond this hard-earned practical knowledge, I've discovered something else. After fifteen years of single life, after shuttling possessions and relationships between a half dozen cracker box apartments, I've found that trees can lead you home. Or at least they can strengthen the fragile bonds between a new family and its home to be.

From the beginning, it was hard not to be smitten by the simple beauty of our nineteenth-century brick farmhouse, with its twelve-pane windows and clean, vertical lines. "A diamond in the rough," the building inspector optimistically called it. However, soon after my wife and I moved in, the house overwhelmed our meager mechanical abilities. Whatever were we thinking? Most people who buy old houses love to fix them up and have a knack for doing so. Or they're rich enough to hire a Bob Vila–caliber restoration crew. But I'm baffled by miter boxes and carpenter squares and have never built as much as a birdhouse.

And so I lived uneasily in the house those first years, drawn instead to the unthreatening emptiness of the old field behind the barn. Out in the tall grass, progress came easier—dig, plant, and water until the living things gradually take hold.

As for the remodeling projects, we finally wised up and befriended a family of affable and affordable Amish carpenters. Their skill and good company have left their own mark on our home, and we're making steady progress on the renovation.

Even so, when the expense and anxiety tempts me to chuck it all and buy a three-bedroom ranch, it's the hunger for homegrown apples and chestnuts that convinces me otherwise. There's clearly an insidious force at work here: Plant and care tenderly for a tree and it will sink its taproot into your soul. Ask persons who have returned, after a few years' absence, to a home they once owned and landscaped. The first words to come from their mouths will likely be, "Wow—look at how big the trees are!" It seems they invested as much of themselves in the trees as they did in the mortgage.

Trees can also help us face our advancing mortality with something other than fear and trembling. It all happens quite unconsciously. Look at a sapling or seedling and you can find yourself wishing away the years and decades. In your mind's eye, you can calculate where today's five-foot red oak will brush the sky in 2030. With enough foresight, you can gaze at a chest-high white pine and envision a little girl nestled in the soft duff of its needles with her dolls and blankets for an afternoon tea party.

Of course, looking that far ahead also prompts some less sanguine questions. In 2030, I'll be seventy-one years old. These trees will have attained the full vitality of adolescence—a healthy white oak can live three centuries—yet what will my own limbs and trunk look like? And this four-acre refuge that's now a peaceful island in a sea of farmland—what's to stop new houses from pressing in on every side? How will our dark, restful evenings survive the encroaching noise and glare of a twenty-four-hour society?

Last week, in a field nearby, a farmer tore out a quarter-mile hedgerow of hardwoods. In a single afternoon, he pushed down far more trees than most of us will plant and nurture in a lifetime. In the face of such destruction, a homemade nursery and windowsill greenhouse seems childishly futile. How can flimsy cardboard cartons withstand the steel-toothed malevolence of a bulldozer?

We all know the cynical, pragmatic answer to that. At the same time, one of the biggest mistakes you can make when planting trees is to think small. Your oak seedlings may look lonely when stuck in the ground at fifteen-foot intervals, but without ample room they'll never have the sunlight and nutrients they need to fully develop. Only through experience and the eyes of faith can we perceive their true potential for growth.

Neither, then, should we limit ourselves to a stunted vision of what our semiwild places, cities, and suburbs can be. As Wendell Berry says, "No life and no place is destitute; all have possibilities of productivity and pleasure, rest and work, solitude and conviviality that belong particularly to themselves."

THE BEST WILD FRUIT YOU
NEVER TASTED

There is perhaps no wild fruit that tastes as good as the service-berry. When the serviceberries ripen in June, it's tempting to gulp them by the handful, grunting all the while like a happy caveman until the purple-red juice dribbles down your chin. I once saw a black bear gorge himself in this fashion along Forest Highway 13 in Michigan's Upper Peninsula. Lost in ecstasy, he was oblivious to the dozen or so camera-clicking tourists nearby.

But be forewarned. As with most unchecked passions, a yearning for serviceberries can make you do things you'll later regret. And this applies equally to humans as well as animals.

In my backyard, there's a young serviceberry tree that for three years had been faithfully watered, pruned, and sheltered from mischievous children. Last spring, for the first time, it bore a hazy cloud of snowy blossoms. You could almost savor the richly sweet berries that would follow. They'd taste like a cross between a cherry and a blueberry, with edible seeds that have a lovely hint of almond.

Or, rather, they would have had it not been for Nemo, our one-year-old black lab. Something about the blossoms waving in the breeze caught his eye. With mindless glee, he charged the tree and snapped off its main trunk. Then he pranced around the yard, the blossom-laden branches waving from his mouth like a tattered flag of spring.

And that did it. Ruining the prize tree was a capital crime, the final offense in a litany of chewed shoes, excavated flowerbeds, and soiled carpets. This time he would really, really have to go. In a deceptively pleasant voice, I lured Nemo into the car and returned him to his previous address—the St. Joseph County Animal Shelter.

That evening my wife was first shocked, then furious.

"I can't believe you took him to the dog pound! People threaten to do that, but they never really *do* it. What kind of man doesn't have room in his heart for a little dog? You can just go sleep on the *couch* tonight!"

Couch? Ouch. Needless to say, during the lonely weekend that followed, I had plenty of quiet time to rethink my domestic priorities. First thing Monday morning, after paying twenty-five dollars in boarding fees, Nemo came back from the shelter for good.

Yet Nemo was certainly on to something. At least he noticed the tree, which is more than most people do. It seems the serviceberry has achieved an interesting status in American society. Although it's widely planted, it's also widely ignored. It is a fruit tree that's become popular for reasons that have nothing to do with its wonderful fruit.

Some of this confusion may arise from its name. Several varieties of serviceberry grow across North America, all of which are in the genus *Amelanchier*. Depending on where you live, the serviceberry may be known as the shadblow, Saskatoon, or Juneberry. In the Upper Peninsula, it's called a sugar plum.

The serviceberry was so named, folklorists say, because it blooms in early spring, when burial rites were once held for the settlers who had died the previous winter. The tree's white blossoms were a sign that it was time to hold funeral "services" since the thawed ground was again soft enough for grave digging.

Whether you know it or not, you've probably seen dozens and maybe hundreds of serviceberry trees. They're all over suburban North America—outside banks, schools, and shopping malls. If you live in a condo or apartment complex, there could be one growing near your window.

Unlike many native species, the serviceberry has been cultivated and used for landscaping. Typically, landscapers are not overly fond of natives. For instance, they find our stately hardwoods too messy (an abundance of acorns and big leaves) or ungainly (a mature white oak can reach three feet in diameter).

By contrast, the native serviceberry is easy to tame. It has four or five slender gray trunks that rise gracefully to form a dense crown of reddish branches. It can be pruned to attain a compact, ornamental shape that tops out at ten to fifteen feet in height. Its small, oval leaves turn ruddy orange in the fall.

In Michigan, the serviceberry typically grows in the understory of mature forests. Wild trees can be forty to fifty feet tall, which makes it hard for humans to reach their fruit. Yet access isn't a problem in most suburban serviceberry plantings, and two of my favorite specimens grow by a parking lot. These citified trees yield more fruit, probably because they benefit from sprinkling systems and lawn fertilizers.

So is it legal to harvest serviceberries (or any other fruit) from trees that grow on public property? I've never heard anyone say you can't. But you can expect some odd looks as you hover around trees whose primary purpose is corporate landscaping. When I'm out gleaning wild edibles during my lunch hour, a typical exchange goes like this.

"Excuse me, sir. What is that you're picking?"

"They're called serviceberries. You wanna try one?"

"Serviceberries? Hmmm—I never heard of 'em. Are they poisonous?"

"No, I try to avoid eating poisonous food. But do you wanna try one?"

At this point, about half of the bystanders will try a serviceberry for themselves. Once they do, they're pleasantly surprised. But how could they not be? Serviceberries have a rich, complex flavor that any gourmand would love. Technically, they're not berries at all but tiny apples rarely larger than half an inch in diameter. Their texture, though, is more like that of a sweet cherry.

On a fruitful tree, it takes about thirty minutes to pick enough serviceberries for a batch of jam. That's considerably longer than it takes to harvest the fruit from, say, an apple tree, from which you can fill a bushel basket in ten minutes or so. Yet a spoonful of serviceberry jam, when lavishly spread on a warm, buttered biscuit, makes the effort expended seem trivial.

There's reason to believe that raising serviceberries could be a new market niche for commercial and small-scale organic growers. Not only are they delectable, but their vitamin C content is ten times greater than that of a blueberry. As a native species, serviceberries resist many diseases that plague other fruits. This means they can be grown with a minimum of herbicides and pesticides.

In western Canada, there's a small but growing market for commercial serviceberry products: jams, jellies, syrups. On Michigan's Keweenaw Peninsula, I bought "sugar plum" jelly at the Jam Pot, a little stand north of Eagle Harbor whose natural products are made and sold by monks of the Holy Transfiguration Skete.

There are you-pick orchards in western Canada but none that I know of in the Midwest. Yet in Michigan's fruit belt, where grapes, apples, peaches, and cherries all flourish, adding a few rows of serviceberry trees to an existing orchard would seem like a good experimental investment. The idea may seem farfetched now, but fifty years ago so did the notion of planting commercial vineyards and building wineries in Michigan. Besides, when it comes to serviceberries, all it takes is that first juicy handful. After that, the funny name becomes unforgettable.

Meanwhile, if you're too proud to pick serviceberries from a parking lot berm outside Wal-Mart, you can always grow your own. On our rural property, we've put in about twenty-five serviceberry trees. Those raised from seedlings (bought for a dollar apiece from the local conservation district) took four years to bear fruit. But the four-foot, forty-five-dollar tree that was purchased at a garden store, *Amelanchier grandiflora,* produced berries the first year. Since serviceberries can vary widely in taste, it pays to find varieties that were bred for their edibility.

Because deer also love serviceberries, you may have to protect small trees until they can grow above the browse line. A circular enclosure of chicken wire, attached to some wooden stakes, works fine for that. Yet around our place, I'm sorry to say, deer are now the only four-legged predators we have to worry about. Nemo left us unexpectedly last summer when he was struck by a car on a foggy August morning.

Nemo was buried in a quiet field east of the house, and by his grave there's a thriving serviceberry sapling. As for the tree that Nemo once attacked, it has made a surprising comeback. Once again, it wears a crown of white blossoms that stir in the breeze like a royal pennant of spring. The berries that follow, it's fair to expect, should have a memorable sweetness all their own.

OSAGE ORANGE

The Tree That Won the Midwest

Across rural southern Michigan, wherever pastures and small farms have faded away, you can see the silvery bones of old fencerows. The still-sturdy wooden posts stand in even ranks even though the barbed wire has long since rusted away.

When I came to the country, I inherited a bonanza of these durable posts, which were stacked in teepee fashion around a big walnut tree. Out in a ramshackle shed, there was also a serviceable roll of fence wire. And since we only needed to build a 20 × 30 dog pen the task seemed easy enough. There was no reason why a reasonably fit guy equipped with college book smarts couldn't build a fence as good as the one some overworked and arthritic old farmer had built thirty or forty years ago.

Suffice it to say that I was rightly chastised for my hubris. The post-hole diggers gave me blood blisters and made my sciatic nerve throb for a week. To get the fence stretched tight I had to use a pickup truck for leverage along with every cuss word my drill sergeant ever taught me.

As for the posts, they were nearly an immobile force of nature. In theory, the fence wire should have been attached to the posts with heavy-duty staples—except that the blasted things were impossible to pound in. It was like trying to hammer a celery stalk into a telephone pole. To make the staples hold fast, I had to first make starter holes with an electric drill (and break several drill bits in the process).

The fence posts weren't made of granite, but I later learned that they were hewn from the next closest thing: Osage orange. If ever a tree was made for fence posts, Osage orange is it. The posts had been outside leaning against a walnut tree for at least twenty years. Yet on most of them the bark hadn't even fallen off. They seemed impervious to decay and certainly to three-quarter-inch fence staples.

My neighbor, a retired farmer, says the posts were cut from a nearby fencerow. They're remnants of a time when Osage orange "hedges" were as much a part of the midwestern landscape as wind-mills and dairy barns. Endless miles of Osage once created thicket-like fencerows along the borders of fields and roadsides.

With its shaggy limbs and thorny branches, the Osage orange (*Maclura pomifera*) has never been a popular yard tree. Nonetheless, it does have some endearingly peculiar qualities. Its smooth, shiny, ovate leaves are a rich shade of dark green, resembling those of a grapefruit tree. And the softball-sized fruit of the Osage is a study in delightful weirdness. Country kids call them hedge apples or monkey brains. They're lime green in color, with a convoluted surface and pulpy center that is indeed brainlike. People can't eat Osage "apples," but deer and squirrels do. If brought inside, they give off a pleasant, citrusy aroma that repels roaches and other insects.

Because of its prevalence in the Midwest, we might assume that the Osage is a native species. But that's not the case. The tree's original range was limited to eastern Texas, Arkansas, and Missouri.

So just how did it become so popular across Michigan and the United States? The answers have to do with aboriginal archery, foot-loose cattle, and the passion of two men to make the boundless prairie a respectable and rectangular place.

For Native Americans, the Osage served a crucial and fundamental purpose: from its sinewy, yellow heartwood, they could make a bow that was powerful enough to kill a buffalo.

As far north as Montana, Osage bows were eagerly sought by tribes of the Great Plains. In 1810, among the Arikara Indians, the going price for these prized weapons was a horse and blanket. French explorers in the Mississippi Valley called the Osage *bois d'arc,* or "bow wood," a name that stuck as the tree's fame moved northward. Even today, a handmade Osage bow will sell for four hundred dollars or more.

During the mid–nineteenth century, white settlers also used the Osage to gain dominion over four-legged creatures. Unlike the plains hunters, however, these agrarian newcomers wanted their herds to stay in one place.

Imagine, for a moment, how the pioneers of the 1850s lived on the nearly treeless grasslands of mid-America. With few fence posts to enclose pastures, they had no choice but to follow their wandering livestock across the open range. Even if posts had been available, the invention of low-cost, mass-produced fencing—barbed wire—was still twenty years away.

Enter John Wright, the editor of *Prairie Farmer,* and his professor colleague Jonathon Turner. For these social reformers, the lack of good fencing on the plains was more than an agricultural problem. It was a roadblock that impeded the order and progress of civilization. It was a barrier that turned upright citizens into free-range nomads. For how could you build schools, churches, and towns when most of the population was forever chasing their cows and sheep across the unpartitioned prairie?

For horticultural salvation, Wright and Turner looked to the Osage orange. Here was a tree that could create a living fence—"horse high, bull strong, and pig tight." Here was a rugged and drought resistant tree that could grow five or six feet in a year. Here was a tree unrivaled as a hedge plant, one that was easily propagated from seed. And if you had to burn your spare fence posts during a harsh midwestern winter? Well, Osage wood gives off more heat than any tree species in North America.

With missionary zeal, Wright and Turner barnstormed the countryside to promote the community-building merits of Osage orange. And they were remarkably successful. Within decades, Osage fencerows were common even in places where fence-post lumber was abundant, such as New England, the Pacific Northwest, and the upper Midwest.

By the early 1900s, the Osage orange had sunk its roots deep into the lore and culture of American life. In the mid-1800s, Osage seed sold for five dollars a pound at a time when prime farmland often sold for around seven dollars an acre. Crews of workers earned a living by traveling the countryside, planting Osage hedges. In 1868 alone, the U.S. Department of Agriculture estimates that more than sixty thousand miles of Osage hedge were planted!

Midwestern farmers learned to plant their corn when Osage leaves "were the size of a squirrel's ear." In winter, farmers and their sons would "cut hedge," thinning the dense Osage fencerows by taking the straight, four-to-six-inch diameter trees that made the best posts. In spring, says my neighbor the retired farmer, they'd use a machetelike hand tool to prune off the trees' side branches. Trimming the trees this way encouraged straight, upright growth.

Of course, what Osage visionaries Wright and Turner could not foresee was the advent of large-scale, mechanized agriculture.

After World War II, farmers moved quickly from horse-drawn plows to high-horsepower tractors. Osage fencerows, once seen as an organizing force of rural civilization, were suddenly obstacles to progress. To create ever larger fields, thousands of hedges were torn out nationwide. Since fewer farmers kept livestock, there was much less need for fence posts. Besides, who wanted the hard, scratchy job of cutting hedge when low-cost steel and treated lumber posts were readily available? (Although an Osage post will stand firm long after treated lumber has dwindled away to wood chips.)

Today, you can still see a few Osage hedges in southern Michigan. They mainly stand along rural roads—provided they don't incur the wrath of highway maintenance crews or interfere with farmers' center-pivot irrigation systems.

But even as the Osage retreats to its native range, I suspect we'll have remnants of its former glory for generations to come. There are still those who value its enduring attributes.

A few years ago, a farmer tore out an Osage hedge near my home in St. Joseph County. The bulldozed heap would have been burned had it not been rescued by several families of Amish farmers. Most of the trees they turned into posts, which will support everything from pasture fences and chicken coops to clotheslines and mailboxes.

Yet the greatest compliment I've seen paid to the Osage was by an Amish carpenter. He took a massive specimen, nearly eighteen inches in diameter, and cut its gracefully curved trunk lengthwise. Then, with the curved halves facing opposite each other, he mounted them flat-side up on sturdy Osage legs. The result is a gorgeous, oval-shaped picnic table that deserves to be in the Smithsonian. Its orange-yellow hue will only grow mellower with age. I'll bet it would fetch twenty-five hundred dollars in a New York furniture store.

Except that it's not for sale. It sits in the woods near a secluded riverbank and a tidy cabin with a new front porch made of Osage orange planks. Which makes me think that Messrs. Wright and Turner were right about the uplifting social influence of their favorite tree. On a Saturday afternoon, I once saw the Osage table buried under a spread of Amish hams, homemade pies, and sugar cookies as big as a draft horse's hoof. Who could ask for anything more civilized than that?

SASSAFRAS

The Savor (and Savior) of Neglected Places

A weed tree. That's what midwestern landscapers, homeowners, and gardeners often call the sassafras. The term *weed* suggests something common and unwanted—a botanical nuisance with no redeeming qualities. And we all know what to do with weeds: spray, dig, hack, and otherwise stomp them out of existence.

When I behold the sassafras, I wonder if we're talking about the same creature. This tree, with its graceful form, which in maturity can resemble the profile of a Chinese pagoda? This tree, whose leaves turn a stunning shade of orange-red and salmon-pink each fall? This tree, whose leaves, bark, twigs, and roots exude an exotic taste and fragrance that's unlike any other in North America?

Furthermore, how can Michiganders disparage the sassafras when its mitten-shaped leaves so clearly resemble the shape of our state? No other tree or state symbol can make that claim, not the Petoskey stone or the brook trout or the Mackinac Bridge. Not even the University of Michigan Wolverines, whose football helmets bear a funky-looking, striped-winged decal that I've never heard anyone properly explain.

It all goes to show how far the sassafras has fallen in the public's esteem. There was a time in American history when the sassafras was avidly sought by kings and conquerors for its unsurpassed medicinal value.

The hype began in 1574 when the Spanish physician Nicholas Monardes lauded the sassafras in his book *Joyfull Newes Out of the Newe*

Founde Worlde (obviously penned before the advent of the spell-checker). As described by Monardes, the sassafras could cure everything from colds and headaches to ulcers and malaria. In those days, any plant with a strong, sweet odor was thought to ward off evil spirits—which most people believed was the real cause of sickness. With sassafras, the aroma comes from safrole oil, a substance also found in spices such as nutmeg and camphor.

By the seventeenth century, speculation in sassafras futures had reached an all-time high. Its perceived healing properties made sassafras the first forest export from the New World. In 1603, British merchants sent a company of men to Long Island, New York, where they spent a month filling the holds of two sailing ships with the bark of sassafras trees. In 1610, sassafras was one of the first exports sent home by Capt. John Smith from the Jamestown colony.

The European sassafras boom eventually went bust after the overblown medicinal claims failed to materialize. Nonetheless, the tree continued to serve an important commercial purpose in the Newe Worlde order.

From the eighteenth century on, sassafras oil was used widely in the United States to flavor soft drinks—that's where the *root* in *root beer* comes from. The taste and aroma of sassafras also enlivened candy, tobacco, and medicine. But its utility ended in 1976, when the Food and Drug Administration (FDA) found sassafras oil to be a mild carcinogen. Apparently, the man-made colorings and sweeteners that have replaced sassafras oil are considered healthier.

For the record, whenever I'm near a sassafras I'll pop one of its tasty twigs into my mouth. Compared to the real hazards of modern life—too much e-mail, driving I–94 in an ice storm—death from an FDA-banned tree substance seems pretty remote. What's more, the sassafras and I have shared roots. My grandmother once swore by sassafras tea as a spring tonic that would cleanse the blood and lift the spirits. That tradition, which she passed on to my father, accounts for one of my favorite childhood memories.

Some dads can make any little trip feel like a great adventure, and I was blessed with one of those dads. As a boy, I recall hiking east of Three Rivers to dig sassafras near a sprawling marsh that my dad called "the cranberries." It was an abundant landscape alive with cottontails, hognose snakes and red-winged blackbirds. Along the railroad tracks we'd hunt for green jewels—the glass insulators that once topped utility poles. We'd pack a sack lunch of bologna and cucumber sandwiches and tromp across old pastures until we found a sassafras thicket. Then, armed with a spade and hatchet, we'd fill a paper bag with sweet-smelling slivers of orange and pink roots.

Back home, weary and footsore, I'd doze on the couch and watch my baseball heroes Al Kaline and Willie Horton patrol the greensward of Tiger Stadium. Meanwhile, dad would steep the roots in an old pressure cooker. "Homemade root beer" was how he optimistically described the finished product. Except our version had no foam, required copious amounts of sugar, and left about an ounce of topsoil stuck to the bottom of the glass. I did feel better but suspect the real tonic had been my father's company and the welcome dose of sunshine after a dreary winter.

I don't know of any grandmothers who still drink sassafras tea—I haven't had any myself in several decades. But, although its pharmaceutical reputation has suffered, the species itself is doing pretty well. That's because the hardy sassafras can thrive in about any fencerow or old field where birds have plopped out the seed of a sassafras berry. (The pea-sized, blue fruits are attractive but inedible to humans.)

And here's where the weed-tree rap comes into play. The sassafras is rightly known as a pioneer species. It's one of nature's storm troopers, part of the wild vanguard that jumps in to reclaim the marginal lands abandoned by humans. It's a mission for which the sassafras is ideally suited. Its roots spread out laterally, and along the laterals other trunks will emerge. That's why it so easily forms thickets in fields and fencerows.

Sassafras trees that grow in thickets are usually stunted. Yet under the right forest conditions they can attain an impressive size. The Michigan champion sassafras, located in Berrien County, is nearly ninety feet tall with a diameter of four and one-half feet. Even a sassafras one-third that size can provide quality lumber. My friend Phil has a stereo cabinet made from sassafras—it is gorgeous wood, orange-brown with golden highlights and a velvety finish. The safrole oil also makes it resistant to insect pests.

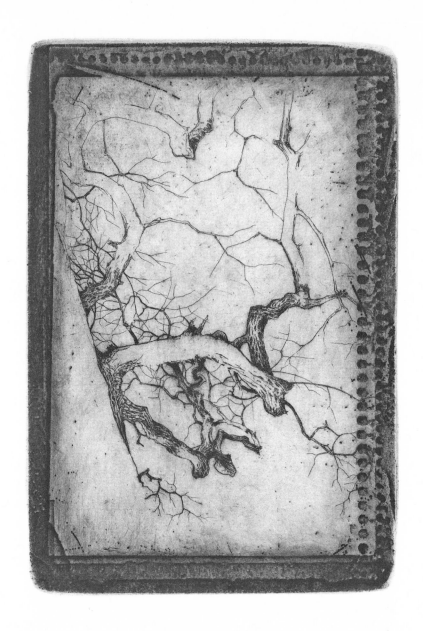

But, even if you can't appreciate the weedy sassafras, at least honor the life force it represents. It's a tree that holds and heals the soil of neglected places, the first act in a drama of natural succession that can culminate in a forest of oak and maple. If we just let it be, the sassafras will do what it's always done: demonstrate nature's power to keep the world sweet, green, and beautiful.

REDISCOVERIES AND REDEPLOYMENTS

ALL THIS AND HEAVEN, TOO

It troubles me now to think that we once took our beautiful, 140-year-old barn for granted. My wife and I bought the farmhouse and barn as a package deal, and, although we marveled at its hand-hewn timber frame and fieldstone foundation, we were ambivalent about its future. We didn't know how or why to save it, nor did we see what purpose a 32 × 50 agricultural building could serve on a "farm" of four acres.

The house was in dire need of renovation first, and it would be at least four years before we could devote ample time and money to the barn. At the same time, we were trying to conceive a child, a frustrating endeavor in its own right. So the unloved barn waited there, full of moldering hay and the rustic and rusted flotsam of the past owner's small-time dairy operation.

As it turned out, we need not have worried at all about the barn's fate. Within the span of a few terrifying minutes, some "young guy with a sexual problem" would solve the dilemma for us.

He paid us a visit about 3:00 a.m. on a cold and still January night. Moments later, after being roused by our barking hound dog, we saw his deviant handiwork. The first thing I noticed was a strange orange glow reflected on the snow-covered field across the road. Then, through the bathroom window, I saw what had caused the glare: the old barn was burning.

It was a terrible yet strangely fascinating sight. The barn's familiar silhouette was stark and ghastly black amid a sea of ferocious flame. I stepped out the back door, and even two hundred feet away the blaze felt warm on my face and neck. An old car that we'd left near the barn was also burning furiously. Sooty flames roared through its heat-shattered windows to envelop the roof and hood.

But the barn—the barn had always been the essence of strength and stability. And now this venerable building and all it stood for was vanishing into memory before us. It was like watching a photograph turn back into a negative. Even at the molecular level, the barn was ceasing to be. In a holocaust of heat and light, the fire was releasing solar energy stored for centuries in timbers and siding cut from virgin Michigan hardwood. The sunshine from pre–Civil War summers was reentering the cosmos in a whirlwind of flame, smoke, ash, and superheated vapor.

This little reverie ended abruptly when I remembered the 250-gallon LP gas tank that sits halfway between the barn and house. It faced the wall of our two-year-old daughter's bedroom. Could the heat make it explode? Could it come crashing through the house like a runaway rocket booster?

"Nance, get Abby!" I yelled through the back door, "we've gotta go now!"

My wife and the hero dog struggled to the car through deep snow, she clutching a bundled child while I could only stare stupefied at the unfolding catastrophe. For all its intensity the fire was oddly quiet, and for that all the more mesmerizing.

We called the volunteer fire department from my brother Jeff's house, a quarter mile away, but we needn't have bothered. By the time they arrived ten minutes later there was nothing to save. The barn's steel roof had acted like a huge reflector oven to hold in all the heat from the burning hay and firewood stored inside. Three hours later, in the grim light of morning, all that remained was a skeleton of charred timbers.

The state fire marshal ruled the fire's cause as arson and nailed an official-looking "$5,000 Reward" sign to a blackened corner post. An arsonist, likely the same one, had earlier the same evening torched a 170-year-old grain mill in Flowerfield about four miles away. I'm almost certain I saw him drive by later in a red Chevy pickup (the same vehicle spotted at the mill fire) to get whatever sick thrill his hobby gave him.

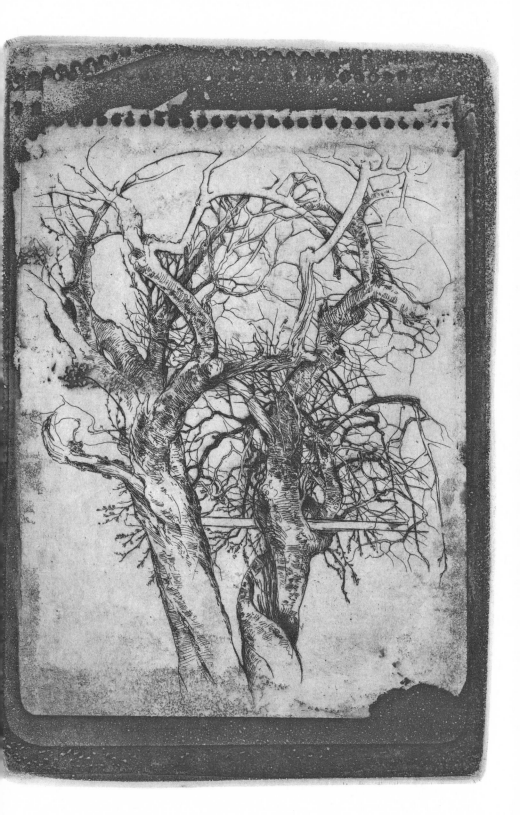

For a few weeks afterward, I entertained some revenge fantasies. A recurring image was that of my wife's late father, a lanky Virginia farmer who once caught a young man stealing peaches from the family orchard. He'd forced the thief to strip naked and, as the mosquitoes buzzed, chained him to a tree—and didn't call the sheriff until morning. A winter version of that punishment, with minor concessions made for hypothermia, seemed like a fair sentence for the arsonist.

Yet, as tempers cooled and clean snow hid the black remains, what we felt most was loss and sadness over the barn's destruction.

Never before had the house stood alone. Since the 1860s, the barn had been the economic hub for a succession of family farms. The previous owners, Delmont and Harriet Freese, moved into the adjacent farmhouse the day after their marriage in 1941—and stayed put for fifty years. Like most small-time farmers, Delmont worked in town to subsidize his agricultural vocation. His real calling was tending a herd of fifteen dairy cows. With a degree of steadfastness that's hard for my generation to fathom, Delmont had milked them twice a day for *four decades.* It probably would have killed him to see what happened on that tragic January night.

After Delmont died, we bought the place from Harriet because we liked the genteel ambience of a brick farmhouse. So on paper the house, barn, and land were legally ours. But we failed to possess the barn in the way that something becomes yours through repeated use, care, and affection. The barn wasn't the epicenter of our livelihood. It was a musty repository for the storage of garden hoses, rakes, and lawn mowers. So why bother to fix the security floodlights or put up a gate by the road? We'd taken the barn for granted, and now, on our watch, it was forever lost to the world.

At the time, I thought the fire marked the end of something. It did, but that was only half true. It was also the opening act in an eighteen-month drama marked by pain, death, war, and finally, rebirth.

What follows is an irregular chronicle of that time when much of what I thought was permanent proved transitory. Through it all, a few lessons became clear. Among them, that our finite universe doesn't waste anything. A dead oak tree, a dying child, a seemingly futile dream—they can all be grist for the re-creation of something else. The hard part, though, was learning to see how a curse can sometimes beget a blessing.

I stand in what was once the barn's granary, ankle deep in cinders and twisted nails that were blanched copper red by the heat. The barn is . . . the barn was. It's all so disorienting. My memories still seem more real than the smoldering heap before me. It's the same confusion that makes us refer to the recently deceased in the present tense: "She loves her grandchildren. . . . He always comes by for coffee on Saturday mornings."

Poking through the ashes, however, makes the loss more tangible. This wasn't just a heap of charcoal but the ruins of a man's life. And nearly all of it spoke of old ways. The barn and its artifacts were a tribute to the horse-drawn, small-scale agriculture that faded away after World War II. Among the remnants were logging chains, harness buckles, grain shovels, pintle hooks, currycombs, corn knives, and muskrat traps. There were plow points and homemade harrows, all well worn and repaired in the jerry-rigged fashion common to miserly farmers who came of age during the Depression. Some of the objects were so personalized by Delmont's use that to touch them now seems voyeuristic, like pawing through a stranger's underwear drawer.

Sentimental value aside, perhaps thousands of dollars in antiques had just gone up in smoke. What ever were we thinking? We should have at least stored the better pieces in our attic or basement. Since we'd never had any of it photographed or appraised, the insurance company would pay nothing for the loss.

A striking example was a fifty-gallon drum that was buried beneath a foot of cinders. It was tucked in the corner of a dimly lit grain bin, and I don't recall seeing it before the fire. When I pried off the lid, it was like opening a Depression era time capsule. Inside was a once-mint collection of muslin feed bags from local grain mills and co-ops. The bags had brand names such as Daily Egg, Red Comb, and Blue Bell and were emblazoned with roosters and suns, wheat heads and corncobs. The bright and cheerful designs on the grain sacks were icons of agrarian plentitude. Framed and matted, you could have made of them an art exhibit. Now they were scorched and water stained, damaged beyond saving. What a colossal waste— another historic treasure whose value the bastard arsonist could never comprehend.

An even bigger loss was a relic that vanished without a trace in the firestorm. It wasn't much, just a pine plank door with a three-inch diameter hole where a doorknob should be. Its character, however, was profoundly human.

To open the door, which led to an animal stall, you reached through the hole and turned a wooden latch. For fifty years, each time Delmont did that he left behind an indelible imprint of his humanity. Over time, the oils from his hand had polished the wood around the hole to a satiny finish. It was a rich shade of nutty brown, fine and lovely as the bowl of a briarwood pipe. The patina of decades had turned this humble door into a testament to Delmont's faithfulness—not to grand ideals or big profits but to his little band of lowing cows and whatever austere dreams sustained him.

If ever a door, or building, had embodied a man's essence, this was it. So in the sense that the barn contained Delmont's spirit I believe it was a haunted place.

And there's something else. The night we moved in I found a light turned on in the shed next to the barn. I was surprised because everything had been locked and the house had sat empty for months. To turn off the light, I had to stand on tiptoe (I'm 6 feet 5 inches tall) and pull a stubby little chain. Since no one had been out there, what made it come on at 11:00 p.m.? My brother is an electrician, and he couldn't explain it either.

I wonder now if it wasn't the old farmer's way of saying goodbye or welcoming the long-awaited newcomers to his beloved home. Because once the mysterious light was turned off the electricity never worked in the shed or barn again.

FEBRUARY ⌒ *Sentimental Journey into Reality*

Despite the fire, the barn's mortise and tenon frame still stands true, masterfully bound with hand-whittled pegs. It takes about an hour of tugging, with logging chains and a sturdy Ford tractor, before it comes creaking and crashing down in a cloud of black dust. An ignoble end for such pioneer artistry, but we had no choice. The ruins were unsafe and had to be razed.

Nonetheless, I felt inspired to make a public display, one that would refute the arsonist and his small-minded vandalism. My first notion was to celebrate the barn that was and make of this hallowed place a rustic shrine. After all, the barn had probably been built on virgin prairie soil. So why not, within the perimeter of the fieldstone foundation, plant a miniature restored prairie to honor the native ecosystem? What a poignant statement that would make.

And why stop there? Why not plane smooth a few of the fire-scarred beams and use them in a new barn as a structural and spiritual link to its nineteenth-century predecessor? Or collect the old pegs and make of them a coat rack for the house? What a grand and noble remembrance this would be.

Alas, the rude realities of middle-class existence prevented such folly. In midwinter, it can cost six hundred dollars a month to heat our house with LP gas, which is why I use the wood-burning fireplace as a supplement whenever possible. To that end, the barn would have to make a sacrificial contribution.

One night, after my brother happened to "stop by" with his chain saw (firewood vulture that he is), we made a useful observation. After cutting open an eight-inch-square timber, we found that the wood was charred to a depth of only half an inch. The timbers couldn't be replaned, as they had too many nails for any sawmill to touch. As cordwood, however, they were ideal. This was perfectly seasoned white oak almost effortless to split with a five-pound maul. It was a lazy countryman's dream: A year's supply of free fuel just two hundred feet from the house. The faithful barn would blaze again and again, but this time its burnt offerings would warm our homes and families.

I did collect about a dozen of the hand-whittled pegs and still carry one around in the front pocket of my winter coat. It's a touchstone of sorts, a totem from home that's a comfort to hold when you're riding on a bumpy airplane. But we don't really need a peg-board coat rack, and I wouldn't know how to build one if we did.

As for the restored prairie, I was partially right: the soil was exceptionally fertile. Except that instead of native wildflowers a patch of exotic weeds quickly sprang up to vanquish the bare earth. The pigweed, quack grass, and foxtail grew taller inside the barn's foundation than anywhere else on the property. Without any human help, this riot of weedy growth soon hid all signs of the fire. As a symbol of nature's resilience in the face of human malevolence, who could ask for anything better than that?

APRIL *Digging Up Bones*

In Southwest Michigan, a green haze of tender buds in the treetops signals the arrival of April. The resurgent sun pries the frost from the chilled earth, and gaudy flights of bluebirds brighten our little pasture.

Spring is also a time of tragic vulnerability. Although wild things are more attuned to their environment than humans, they, too, make fatal miscalculations. A newborn lamb can perish in an April snow squall despite the frantic licks of its mother's tongue. Fruit trees and plants that leaf out and blossom too soon are punished for their insolence by the killing frosts of May.

For some cosmic reason, spring has also been a fertile season for my wife and me. Our first child was conceived during the first week of April, and in early April 2001, after two trying years of trying, we were for the second time successful. It was a joyful time for us both, with tulips blooming near the porch and the promise of another Christmas baby in the making. But, with the larger problem solved, another unsettled issue reared its head. Specifically, the nineteenth-century shortcomings of the house where we planned to raise our family.

When we bought the place, it seemed cool and earthy to have an upstairs that lacked plumbing and central heat. Indeed, apart from a few stray electrical outlets, the second story had changed little since the Civil War. Having hung out at several hippy farmhouses in the 1970s—the Golden Age of homegrown everything—I rather appreciated that ambience. The trouble is I never asked my wife what she thought of indoor temperatures that hovered in the midthirties during the cold days of winter.

"We're young, healthy, and like to camp," I said, "so why not pitch our tent upstairs, so to speak, for the winter?"

She angrily rejected that analogy along with the very idea that she could be forced to live under such backward circumstances. Had I forgotten that she'd grown up in a meager farmhouse like this one? Did I realize how mortified she'd been by her bedroom, which had blankets and plastic taped forlornly to the drafty windows? As a child, she'd vowed never to live that way again. And now, after four years of college and six years of marriage, she'd moved back to the same small town and was living once more in a cruddy farmhouse.

To make matters worse, for the last two years we'd kept our queen-sized bed in the living room while our daughter slept in the one downstairs bedroom. This hillbilly flophouse arrangement had become a family embarrassment. Yet, with a second child on the way, we still couldn't afford the necessary repairs to make the upstairs livable.

Then, just as it had nurtured untold generations of four-legged newborns, the barn's maternal spirit saw us through. The insurance company had agreed to pay full replacement costs for the building's contents. In other words, they'd pay today's prices for *all* the items destroyed by the fire. This included our belongings and the odds and ends that were in the barn when we bought it.

With renewed vigor, I sifted through the cinders to resurrect every identifiable object that we could add to the insurance claim. Grain shovels, milking buckets, an ancient cement mixer; it all counted! From this secondhand salvage, we'd get a big enough check to remodel and heat the upstairs. Depart now from our midst ye demons of childhood scarcity.

After this final act of cannibalization, there was no more for the barn to give. We'd picked clean its bones. All that was left was to inter the remains.

JUNE ℰ℧A Midsummer's Night Tragedy

On a cloudless June day I drove my cousin, Steve, to Wrigley Field in Chicago to watch the Cubs play the Cardinals. Summer traffic is murderous in the city, but this annual excursion is always worth the effort. Since Steve uses a wheelchair, we are entitled to park a hundred feet from the stadium and sit in VIP/handicapped seats behind home plate. If memory serves correctly, the Cubs won and Mark McGwire homered for the Cards.

And that, effectively, was the end of summer. When I arrived home at 9:30 p.m., happily tired and sunburned, I was met at the door by my trembling wife.

"I started bleeding a few hours ago, and now it's getting worse."

Miscarriage? It wasn't a word, or possibility, to which I'd given a second thought. Conception was supposed to be the hard part. After that, pregnancy was a failsafe process whose successful outcome was assured by the safeguards of modern medicine.

Thirty minutes later I knew better.

I was sitting by Nancy's bed in an emergency room as a beeping monitor announced that her blood pressure was dropping rapidly. "My God," I thought, looking around at the understaffed small town hospital, "my wife could bleed to death in here."

She didn't, of course, but someone else had. A tiny heart had beaten its last; an unknown soul had fled back to whatever realm it had come from.

"If you want to take a look," the doctor said, "it's over there."

No, that would not be necessary.

No, I did not want to bear in my memory the image of such tragic desecration.

And, no, I did not need what TV psychologists call therapeutic "closure." I just wanted my wife to get better so we could leave because she wanted to cry, and needed to cry, but was too sick and scared to do it in a hospital.

On our way out, the distracted nurse handed us a brochure entitled "Coping with Miscarriage." The images depicted in it were stick figures, that genderless, moon-faced species that have inhabited government health care materials since the 1970s. The nurse was doing her job, but under the circumstances her gesture seemed grossly inadequate.

The emergency room physician, who was genuinely kind, could only say that this was "nature's way." The bad seed had been expelled.

"But now," said my wife, crying softly, "I'm not going to have a baby."

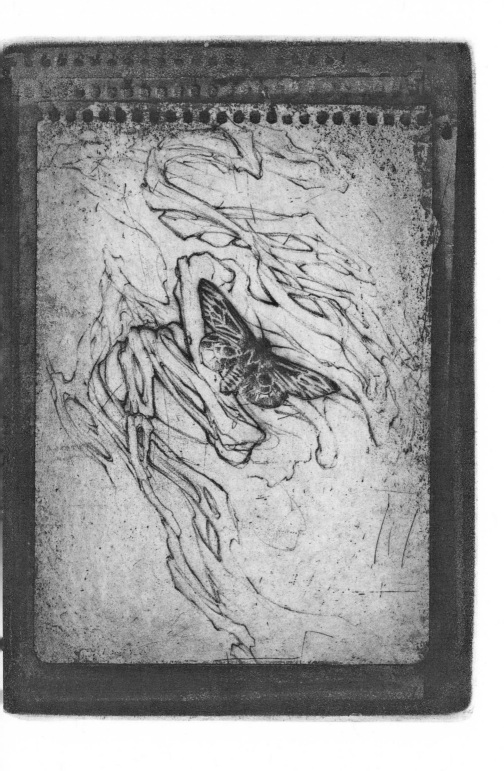

When I retold the story the next afternoon, I was leaning on a shovel next to a John Deere bulldozer.

"Damn. That's too bad. I'm real sorry to hear it," said my good neighbor, Bones, who I'd hired to bury the barn's rubble. "But when it happens they say it's for the best."

So I've heard. Although what more could he say? Besides, dozer work is expensive and I was paying him by the hour.

As the day wore on, I busied myself with gathering up the usable fieldstone. All the while, the dozer roared and the pit grew like a raw wound in the earth. A new excavation is usually the sign of fresh beginnings, yet this one was a reminder of things lost and hopeless.

By evening, all that remained was a pile of scrap timber. It wasn't in a good location for a bonfire, but I wanted nothing more than to burn it. I needed to burn it, had to burn it, and didn't want to stop with the pile. I wanted to obliterate every sign of the accursed barn along with my futile, stillborn striving to make of this place a country retreat. So what if the flames melted the power lines overhead? What did I care if they ignited the hayfield nearby?

Heat lightning flashed in the western sky, but the clouds never begrudged more than a few stray sprinkles. Yet on toward midnight, as the fire petered out, I felt too tired for rage or revenge. The storm had passed, and the words of the old Ash Wednesday blessing came to mind: "Remember, man, that you are dust and to dust you will return." Well, at least these ashes I could honor. As for the flesh of my flesh, where was he now, this child we would call Anthony Michael? And what kind of father was I, who would bury a barn but not his unborn son?

JULY ☙ *A Hero's Untimely End*

All visible signs of the barn fire are gone, but the bad mojo unleashed by the arsonist lingers on.

The week after we lost the baby, I was walking Spot when a coon and her three cubs crossed the road in front of us. Raccoons are excellent climbers and swimmers, but on foot they look humorous and awkward. It was especially comical to see the young ones imitate their mother's waddling, hump-backed gait. They were a furry little caravan intent on a twilight raid to the big watermelon field next door. Except instead of enjoying a meal they were about to become one.

For Spot, coons are for killing, and there was no stopping him. He lit into the cubs with a sickening fury that sent them tumbling and yelping toward the edge of the road. Next he turned on the mother, who stood hissing on her hind legs with the ferocity of a cornered grizzly. Spot jumped back for a moment, startled by her bravery. Then his treeing instincts prevailed, and he drove the sow coon to the top of a nearby cottonwood. I went to check on the cubs but they were all dying, their short lives oozing away on the warm pavement. I had tried to restrain Spot but once again was unable to help the helpless.

Spot's turn came a few weeks later. He'd always barked and growled at strangers, which isn't a bad trait for a country dog. Lately, though, Spot's bad temper had grown unpredictable. He'd nipped at our daughter a few times, a serious offense that should have warranted his removal. Then, while we were on vacation, he bit—on successive days—two of the nephews who were there to feed and walk him. These were kids he knew and liked. How could we ever trust him again around children?

And yet we loved him dearly. He did goofy things like sleep in a wheelbarrow, eat cucumbers from the garden, and howl with lovesick abandon when I played my harmonica. For the first four years of marriage, we had called Spot our "dog child" and lavished on him the excess attention that childless couples often give their pets.

Now there was nothing to do but have him put down. We were still on vacation when the dogcatcher came to get him. So we never said our good-byes, difficult as that would have been. As a result, Spot's absence never seemed final. It's like he simply ran off again, as he'd do for a few days every March or April when the musky aromas of spring stirred his hound dog wanderlust to a frenzy.

The year's losses were mounting, and the old urge do something meaningful resurfaced. As a living tribute, I decided to plant a hickory seedling along the pasture fencerow. It leafed out briefly but, predictably, wilted and died while I was away on business. I left it there anyway. Somehow, the sight of its tiny, shriveled trunk has brought a measure of filial comfort. Perhaps closure is more important than some of us care to admit.

SEPTEMBER ✑ *In Defense of Things Local*

Weather permitting, I like to take a ten-minute stroll before bedtime down the little-traveled road that runs parallel to our home. It's good medicine for unburdening one's mind of the cares of the day.

During my evening walk on September 10, 2001, I watched an eastbound jet course through the sky overhead. I recall thinking how fragile, how vulnerable its occupants truly were. All of them borne aloft in a fragile cocoon of steel that thundered along at the speed of sound through the deadly cold of the stratosphere. It seemed so perilous, so unnatural. I said a prayer for them and their safety; certainly not the first time I or anyone else has done such a thing. So I'm not sure if my impulse, which was especially strong that night, was born of coincidence or prescience.

What is certain, of course, is how the next day's tragedies instantly made us all feel violated and fearful. The dogs of war were unloosed, and it looked as though they would never be leashed again in our lifetime. But, as selfish and terrible as this may sound, the weeks that followed 9/11 did me a world of good. As a member of the National Guard, I suddenly had something bigger than my own problems to think about.

I'd been in the guard for more than twenty years and was actually set to retire in a few months. I was eager to reclaim the forty annual days of training that peacetime service in the guard requires. I wanted to plant a big garden and take blissful retreats at monasteries. Yet after 9/11 such middle-aged diversions seemed silly and shallow. This was no time to run off and play gentleman farmer on my orange lawn tractor. Serving in the military, even part time, made me feel important—which Freud described as the greatest human need of all. In the interest of my ego as much as national security, I extended my enlistment for another year.

MID-OCTOBER ✑ *Stagnation Begets Inspiration*

My post-9/11 duty was never difficult or dangerous. In the twilight of my guard career, I'd taken a magazine editor's job at a public affairs unit in Lansing. We mainly took phone calls from civilian reporters who were as mystified about the military as the military is about them. By the time American bombs and missiles began raining down on Afghanistan, I'd nearly forgotten the lesser act of terrorism that had leveled our barn.

Then, in mid-October, I got a call from Joe, an Amish friend who's a carpenter. "A guy just canceled on a house framing job, so I've got an opening," he said. "I think we can build you a barn by Christmas."

I wasn't sure what to say. After the barn burned in January, I told Joe I'd like him to build us another one someday. Given his workload, I didn't think our turn would come for at least a year. In truth, about the last thing I wanted yet this year was to manage a construction project. I had neither the time nor mental energy for it. Since Joe and his five-man Amish crew don't drive, I'd have to get up at 5:00 a.m. and make a one-hour round trip to get them *before* I began my forty-five-minute commute to work.

And the larger, still unanswered question was whether a new barn was necessary. To paraphrase Gloria Steinem, we needed a barn like a fish needs a bicycle. Our "farm" consisted of one cat, two guinea hens, a small garden, and several hedgerow plantings of little trees. Surely, our agricultural storage needs could be met by a spacious new garage. Wouldn't it be nice, on a wintry morning, to climb in a car without first scraping a quarter inch of frost from the windshield?

Then there was the kitchen, with its leaky sink, tiny stove, hideous linoleum floor, and peeling wallpaper. It was last remodeled in the 1960s by a farm wife whose decorating ideas were limited to the beige spectrum.

On the other hand, we did have a decent insurance settlement check still in hand. It was unlikely that we'd ever have so much cash in our savings account again. So, if not now, when?

And, if not this dream of a hobby farmer's paradise, which has dogged me my entire life, then what: a cement driveway and a remote-control fireplace in the suburbs? With my deskbound office job, I already had all the starched-shirt convention I could stand. A small farm, with its attendant joys and sorrows, seemed like a healthy antidote to middle-class drudgery. And, unlike the military, one could indulge his avocation without leaving home.

First, though, we'd need a barn.

"Sounds good," I told Joe. "When can you begin?"

EARLY NOVEMBER ✐ *Sex, Fires, and Measuring Tape*

It's 6:30 a.m., and a mile away the Willingham's barn is burning. Even through a screen of trees, I can see the orange fireball. It's as if the morning sun has risen wrongly in the north.

I don't know the couple well, but after work I stop by to commiserate. The barn is a smoking shambles, and the intense heat has blistered the vinyl siding on their nearby garage.

"We loved this old barn, that's really what sold us on the place," said Mrs. Willingham, running her fingers distractedly through her hair. "My husband, he spent all summer fixing and painting the roof, and now . . . now this. It's just . . ."

Stupid? Unfair? Pointless? Terrifying? Oh, yes, it's all of those. Their barn, like ours, had stood near the road, making it an easy target for the local arsonist. Still, it could have been worse. The night before was unseasonably warm, so the Willinghams had let their horses stay out in the pasture. Otherwise they'd have been roasted alive.

Out of curiosity, I call the county prosecutor to see out how the "investigation" is proceeding. It's not. Nothing's been done. This despite three neighborhood fires within the last nine months that were all ruled as arson. Since no one's been killed, the police and sheriff won't commit the manpower necessary to investigate the crimes.

"Well," I ask the prosecutor, "can you at least tell me what kind of person would do this?"

"Oh, it's usually some guy in his twenties or early thirties with a sexual problem. Though it could be a woman. In the mid-1980s, we had a string of barn fires near Centreville. It turned out they were started by this gal who was having an affair with a volunteer fireman. She'd start a fire, he'd get called out, and then they'd sneak off for a little rendezvous. She got careless, and we finally caught her."

A fascinating psychological profile, but at this point it doesn't really matter. Firebug love trysts and sexual deviants be damned. I'm going to rebuild.

The first step seems so insubstantial. With a tape measure and a can of orange spray paint, I plot off the new barn's location: It will be 32 × 36 feet on a patch of unbroken sod. I mark the corners with field-stones left over from the old barn's foundation.

What comes next is pure joy. At the kitchen table, I sketch on graph paper what I think the new barn should look like. It's no less than the future of this place, a building that I hope will stand for 150 years. It's so much fun that it should be illegal, and were I designing a commercial building it would be. I have no qualifications. What I know of drafting I learned in an eighth-grade shop class. But since it's a barn I can do this part of the job myself. Joe will calculate the roof pitch, truss dimensions, and other technical details.

The design ideas are a composite culled from the twenty or so old barns that I pass each day on the way to work. All were built in the late nineteenth century and the early twentieth. They are structures of considerable beauty, durability, and function, examples of what textbooks call "vernacular architecture." It's likely that most, if not all, of them were built by men who never advanced beyond grade school. They learned their trade through apprenticeship and exam-ple. They were masters of improvisation who capably used whatever local materials were available. In nearby Cass County, there's a mas-sive barn that was sided with the wood milled from one enormous tulip poplar tree.

Ours would be an authentic, wooden frame barn, not a sheet-metal pole building. Even so, some compromises are necessary. The footings and foundation would be poured concrete instead of split fieldstone (only the rich can afford masons who still do that work). For the side walls, instead of hardwood planks over a full timber frame there would be cedar plywood over 2 x 6 inch studded side-walls. One-inch wooden strips, nailed vertically at one-foot inter-vals, would lend it the "board and batten" appearance of traditional barn siding. And this barn, unlike the old model, would have as its crowning glory a gambrel or hip roof. The hip roof would give it the bread loaf shape that most people associate with the word *barn*.

And, whereas the old barn had just three windows, this one would have twenty—at least four to a side. The light would shine in darkness, and hopefully the darkness would not overcome it.

What a change in perspective the year's events had wrought. When we bought the house, I wasn't a barn lover. They seemed like the ultimate rural cliché, the trite mainstay of bank calendars and department store wall art. Now there were books about barns stacked on my nightstand. No longer could I look upon a dilapidated barn as quaint or picturesque. I saw only leaky roofs, unglazed windows and crumbling foundations that cried out for repair. I saw neglected cultural relics whose owners had failed to protect the treasures entrusted to them by posterity.

NOVEMBER *Song of the Saw and Hammer*

When an Amish crew builds your barn, you often get to see where the wood comes from. In this case the source was Hostetler's Sawmill, an Amish-owned business where a diesel generator powers the equipment. When I arrive to pick up my order, they're still cutting away, feeding red oak and tulip poplar logs into a howling, three-foot buzz saw. Seconds later, a couple of ruddy Amish teenagers—no safety glasses, hard hats, or earplugs in sight—load the lumber on my trailer. My generation, raised as we were in the prepackaged and plasticized world of the 1960s and 1970s, loves this kind of stuff. Deprived of authentic contact with nature, we now yearn for things rough cut and unrefined.

We prefer clothes and building materials that are nubbly, grainy, bumpy, and as infinitely textured as an old wino's nose. Our jeans have been bleached and beaten into limp servitude before we even try them on. Our new coffee tables have been "distressed" with ballpeen hammers and flailed with car keys. You won't catch us brushing a thick coat of varnish over the rough bricks of a fireplace, as my grandmother suggested that I do to mine: "But dear, don't you think things look better when they're shiny?"

The Amish use rough-cut lumber because it's sturdy, cheap, and readily available. They don't need to reconnect with their inner druid. On Joe's farm, there are draft horses, carriage horses, pigs, goats, chickens, sheep, cats, an entire softball team of children, and a huge garden that could feed a rifle company of Marines. You can't help but encounter (or step in) unrefined nature at every turn.

Even so, there *is* something wonderfully substantial about a sixteen-foot plank of oak that's two inches thick, twelve inches wide, and weighs more than a hundred pounds. "When we're building a barn out of native, the guys start to complain by the end of the day," says Joe, always a master of understatement. I loaded some of the rough-cut lumber myself, and my neck was stiff for a week.

Most magnificent, however, are the timbers that will stand at the barn's center. They arrived today on my neighbor's flatbed trailer, and the load was so heavy he was afraid to cross the Langley Covered Bridge. The sixteen- and eight-foot beams are little more than square trees with the branches and bark shorn off. Rosy red, redolent with the half-sweet scent of oak, they'll become a skeleton on which the barn (and my dreams of rural nirvana) will be enfleshed.

When used in its most natural form, lumber can certainly give buildings a spiritual dimension that's lacking in your average strip mall. In the world's religious traditions, trees often stand at the center of things. In the Christian hereafter, as described in the Book of Revelation, the Tree of Life grows alongside a crystal river that flows from the throne of God (heavenly citizens can partake of its fruit, unlike its verboten counterpart in the Garden of Eden). In Norse mythology, the roots and branches of Ygdrassil, a mighty ash, cover the world and uphold the universe. For the Egyptians, a holy sycamore guards the threshold between life and death. And it was under a bodhi tree that Buddha found enlightenment after seven weeks of meditation.

At first, none of the barn's woody spiritual eminence is visible from the road. For the first week after Joe's crew poured the floor and footings, the building resembled any other garage under construction.

That changed when the roof trusses began to rise above the second story. Again, the imagery that comes to mind is religious, and it would be hard for even a nonbeliever to see it otherwise. The thirteen handmade trusses—creamy white against the cobalt winter sky—do look like slender fingers clasped in prayer. And it's no coincidence that the barn's traditional upright form resembles that of a church. In Europe, many of the earliest barns were built on the same basilican floor plan as medieval cathedrals. They had an aisle, a nave, a transept, and even buttressed arches. These tithe barns served as banks, storing the 10 percent contributions of grain that churches required from their parishioners. While the function of barns has evolved, much of their original shape has not.

So up it goes—a church in barn's clothing, a wooden building that's already an anachronism in its own right. But there's a price to pay here, and it's not just by me, the guy with the overspent checkbook. It's the crew, working outdoors in cruel winter weather, that must suffer for its daily bread.

In early December, southern Michigan is cold and damp, with a chill that penetrates your bones like a virulent strain of arctic flu. Joe's rule is that they'll work outside if it's no colder than ten degrees. If it's windy, twenty degrees is the cutoff point. Although a ton of lousy weather can blow through that self-imposed window, in eight weeks the crew missed only a few days. Without complaint, they'd sleepily emerge from the womb of my warm car and head straight for the half-finished barn, where frost-rimmed stacks of lumber and frozen tool belts await.

The young ones, their clean-shaven faces pinched red by the wind and cold, climbed forty-foot extension ladders to nail on siding and rafters. These guys are all avid outdoorsmen, some of them up at 4:00 a.m. each day to run their traplines. When they come down from a roof because their hands are too frozen to grasp a hammer, you know they're doing work that would kill about 95 percent of the population. But they always go back up, shouting down measurements and wisecracks to the older guys below, whose bad backs and creaky knees keep them on the ground manning the saws and miter boxes.

One morning, a forty-something crew member confided that this might be his last winter. "I tell you, I don't think I can take this cold much longer," he said. "I go home at night so stiff and tired I can hardly move. I don't want to work in the trailer factory, but my wife's going blind and there's doctor bills to pay."

For an Amishman, that's saying a lot. Shared work is a central tenet of Amish life, and the crew enjoys the challenge and friendship of building barns more than anything except farming. Still, the plants of northern Indiana beckon. The region is the nation's leader in recreational vehicle and modular home manufacturing, and Amish workers—reliable, industrious, and drug-free—are always in demand.

The men speak of these factory jobs with sad resignation, rarely failing to mention the tradeoff between stable employment and lost personal fulfillment. To work so much among the English (their term for non-Amish) weakens their communal bonds of language, faith, and culture.

The irony is that Joe and his crew could charge half again as much and still have more than enough work. But they won't. Their fees are based on their community's idea of what a fair wage should be—and they're not in this world to get rich.

Of course, their generosity and handshake contracts can backfire. The crew also hires out for framing and roofing jobs, and sometimes it gets shafted by crooked contractors. In such cases, I don't know who to feel sorrier for, the short-changed Amish or the person whose heart is so small and mean that he would cheat these honest men.

For our part, we provide what hospitality we can. We leave the house open, and I stoke up the backroom fireplace each morning. They come tromping in at 10:00 a.m. for a break, hoo-hooing from the cold and joshing around in their native German tongue. It's only fitting that wood from the old barn should blaze in the hearth to warm those who are building a new one. In lieu of the arsonist's apprehension, poetic justice will have to suffice.

The idea of working for less—when someone would gladly pay you more—is intriguing to say the least. Most of us scheme and cajole for every nickel we can get. Still, what would happen if the desire to make more money ceased to be our primary motivation? Would doing work well for its own sake, without expectation of great reward, allow nobler virtues to develop? Can even menial tasks become, as the Amish believe, a route to sanctification and spiritual growth?

In the new barn, there's a railing that runs alongside the stairs that lead to the hayloft. For such a utilitarian purpose, Joe could have easily used a standard two-by-four. Instead, he took a fifteen-foot length of straight-grained tulip poplar and made a masterpiece. How much time he spent planing, sanding, and routing this thing is anybody's guess. It's silky smooth and deftly rounded to fit the human hand. People say "Oooh!" when they touch it, as if running their fingers over a mink coat.

It's easy to picture Joe at work on that cold, gray day. His beard's flecked with little curls of wood shavings, and the new barn echoes with the whine of saws and the thunderclap of hammers. As the foreman, there's much for Joe to supervise and worry about, but he's focused on this one thing—an anonymous piece of carpentry indistinguishable from hundreds of other objects he's made this year. Somehow he finds the time to do even a little job right.

In my own career, I've often heard myself or others say, "It all pays the same" or "It's good enough for government work" or "Six months from now, who's going to care?" Deep down, though, I suspect few of us really believe that. We want our jobs to have a good and lasting impact on the world. We want our talents and skills to promote order, peace, happiness, and healing. We want people to value our work the way an old man in 2025 might as he huffs up his hayloft stairs and leans confidently on a smooth and sturdy handrail that was made more for love than money.

JANUARY ‿ Turning Over the Keys

Thanks to our new barn, we won't need to buy any tree mulch this year. When you use rough cut lumber, there's an endless amount of planing and fitting involved. This explains why yellow and pink drifts of sawdust cover the barn floor up to two feet deep in some places. Before the cleanup is over, I haul out twenty-three wheelbarrows full.

But untreated lumber does have its drawbacks. As we unloaded some of the planks, a handful of black specks spilled on the ground like peppercorns. They were, in fact, hibernating carpenter ants whose main function in life is to eat wood. Had the wood been kiln-dried, they would have perished. Instead, it's likely that even more ants remain hidden inside one of the big beams, slumbering away oblivious to their new location. When they awaken in spring, I'll be waiting with a jug of insecticide. I believe in a sustainable world, but no freeloading ants are gonna eat my barn.

All the same, the barn is nearly finished. I picked up the crew today for the last time, all of us squeezed into my four-door Olds sedan, which seemed spacious before I started hauling around five well-fed Amishmen.

At 3:30 p.m., Joe called me at work (from my phone) with a final question. The lumberyard was out of steel latches for the stalls and could he fashion them out of wood? Of course. When Joe gets an urge to build something unusual from wood, you let him. I suspect he could carve a pair of socks from a four-by-four. The result was a remarkable, P-shaped latch that falls automatically into place when you close the stall door. It looks deceptively easy to design, and therein lies its genius.

The next day the job was finally complete, and it was time for a ceremonial walk-through. As we stood in the quiet barn, I sensed some reluctance on Joe's part, a hesitancy to let go. At first, I thought there was something wrong, perhaps some major miscalculation on the materials bill.

That wasn't the case at all. It gradually dawned on me that Joe simply needed time to say good-bye to his creation. After all, I just foot the bill. It was he and his crew who transformed a horizontal pile of lumber into an edifice of beauty and might.

This is the third construction job the crew has done for us, and when they draw to a close I always feel a bit melancholy myself. No more early mornings on Amish farms, savoring the aromas of wood smoke and homemade sausage. No more lantern-lit searches in old sheds to hunt down wayward tools or inspect gleaming racks of coon, fox, and muskrat hides. No more Homeric tales of runaway horses or spirited discourses on the merits of mousies versus wax worms as the best bait with which to catch perch through the ice.

Once again they left me with no recourse.

"Say, Joe," I mention on the drive home, "did I ever mention this idea I've got for a timber-framed garage?"

As it turned out, there was one more administrative hurdle to clear before the barn was officially ours. The mortgage company held our final insurance payment in escrow and wouldn't release it until its building inspector had examined the finished project. I wasn't home during his visit, but Nancy filled me in at the dinner table.

"So, did he say anything about the craftsmanship and how much we got for our money?" (That's me—always fishing for a compliment.)

"No, he just asked why there wasn't any insulation and why it wasn't painted."

It seems the young man was a bit baffled. He was a product of the Detroit suburbs, and nowhere in his building inspector course had they covered agricultural buildings. My usually soft-spoken wife, raised as she was on a working farm, does not suffer such fools gladly. Their conversation apparently went something like this.

Inspector: Why isn't there any insulation in here?
Wife: What?
Inspector: There's no insulation. Won't it get cold in here?
Wife: Yes, in the winter.
Inspector: But some people like to store things at a warm temperature. Aren't you going to heat it?
Wife: This is a barn. You don't heat barns. They're for animals and hay and tractors and firewood. You want to keep something warm, you store it somewhere else.
Inspector: OK. But I also see the barn's made of bare wood.
Wife: Uh-huh.
Inspector: So why isn't it painted?
Wife: "Why . . . isn't . . . it . . . painted?
Inspector: Yeah, it's not really finished until it's painted.
Wife: We're in Michigan, and its January.
Inspector: Yeah?
Wife: How many people paint barns when it's twenty degrees outside?

Weighty questions, indeed. Nevertheless, the young building inspector dutifully mailed us his report a few days later. It pronounced that "the barn was 98 percent complete—except for paint."

JUNE ～ Barn Again

The honey-hued barn sits curing in the sun like an overturned sailing ship that somehow washed up in the backyard. In a few weeks, it will be ready to paint. The inside smells wonderfully of new wood, and it's as clean swept and uncluttered as it will ever be.

As I soon discover, an empty barn is a vacuum to which the spare possessions of the world are inexorably drawn. "Come unto me," the barn seemed to say, "all you friends and relatives who are overburdened with consumer goods." Within a few months, this virginal space was filled with stuff that was largely not our own: a good friend's pontoon boat and my brother-in-law's spare furniture, hot tub, and exercise machine.

Deep in the American psyche there's also an expectation that a new barn deserves a party. This idea was suggested to me by several people who neither had barns nor had ever been to a barn party (including an ethnic Chinese coworker who was raised in Singapore). Although we're not entertaining types, my wife and I agreed that a celebration would be a great way to vanquish the gloom of our recent past.

Indeed, the "Barn Again Party" would be an occasion of unabashed happiness. That's not something easy to say out loud because we stoic midwesterners consider it bad form to act unduly happy in public. Even on a splendid Indian summer day, it's unseemly for us to get exuberant about the fine weather. "Yeah, but we'll pay for this!" is the typical reply. As if we'll be punished by a long, cold winter because we had the temerity to enjoy autumn's beauty.

But on June 1, the day of the party, there's more to celebrate than nice weather and a new barn. For since the magical month of April Nancy had again been pregnant.

We let the first trimester pass quietly before announcing the news. The ultrasound shows no problems, only a Christmas baby floating blissfully in its amniotic nursery. Thanks to the old barn's bounty, he or she will soon have a new and frost-free upstairs bedroom. With cosmic efficiency, it seems the arsonist's misdeeds have been turned against him. There's also a new black lab pup that stays in the yard and loves to play with children (but not taste them).

As for the party itself, it was everything we dared hope it would be. We invited about a hundred neighbors, friends, family members, and, of course, the barn builders. We borrowed folding tables from the church and filled them with homemade picnic food. We grilled buffalo burgers and hot dogs and ate trays full of Amish-made pies, doughnuts, and cookies. There was a plastic wading pool filled with ice, pop, and plenty of cheap American beer—whatever was on sale at Sam's Club.

In the spiky stubble of a freshly mown field, barefoot Amish kids played kickball with my cousins and nieces. In front of the big sliding door, a bluegrass band played unplugged music that was perfect for a new barn, a lawn chair audience, and the lingering, turquoise twilight of a summer evening. Until dusk, the clink of tossed horseshoes and laughter drifted across the weedy expanse where the old barn once stood.

For those few hours, joy and love were again triumphant. We knew, of course, that more war, sickness, death, and uncertainty would follow. We knew this new barn, and everything and everyone in it, would pass away. But this moment also seemed to foreshadow better things to come; a traveler's dispatch, as it were, from an undiscovered country.

It was an intimation best explained by a white-haired widow who sought me out as she left that evening.

"I want to thank you so much. The party was wonderful and the barn's beautiful and you have a fine family. All this," she added, as if recalling a favorite memory, "all this and heaven, too."

IN LAND TRUSTS WE TRUST

Any midwesterner who loves nature and spends much time in the near suburban countryside will eventually have this experience.

While traveling the back roads, you happen upon a little woods or lovely farm. It could be the first time you've seen it or it could be a place you've secretly admired for years. Normally, you'd slow down below the posted speed limit to savor the view. You'd scan the forest floor for patches of spring wildflowers. You'd fantasize about living in the white clapboard farmhouse and about blissful autumn walks down a gravel lane that's arched with friendly old sugar maples.

Except this time, instead of the usual peaceful easy feeling, a lump of anxiety clenches your throat. For in the midst of your Norman Rockwell daydream someone has planted a For Sale sign.

It's as if the stench of commerce has seeped into the sanctuary. All that's beautiful now seems fragile, even tragic, because you know what kind of environmental carnage a For Sale sign—and those little pink surveyor's flags—can foreshadow. So, more than anything, you're smitten with the urge to rush in like an avenging earth goddess and wrest this land from the iron maw of destruction. The fact that you're driving a ten-year-old car and struggling to pay your current mortgage makes this impossible dream seem all the more righteous—and frustrating.

"It's just not *right!*" you mutter through gritted teeth. "How come it's paunchy developers with bad comb-overs and silky golf shirts that get to buy all the beautiful land? Who authorized *them* to turn our countryside into a ChemLawn monoscape?!"

The short answer is that developers know how to convert little woods and lovely farms into quarter-acre lots and cul de sacs that quickly earn millions of dollars in revenue. This skill makes developers quite popular with bankers and real estate brokers, many of whom are endlessly preoccupied with making large sums of money.

For us commoners, however, the larger question is still valid: what can an average person do to protect at least a few wild places in his or her community from development? In other words, save them from becoming yet another strip mall, gas station, or lackluster housing complex that's clad entirely in beige vinyl siding.

There is indeed a practical way to help preserve the wild and local places around us. There is a certain kind of nonprofit organization that's adept at doing just that.

But first, based on my failed experience as the Lone Green Crusader, let me explain how *not* to do it.

After graduating from college in 1988, my plan was simple. I'd land a decent job, live frugally in a beige vinyl-sided apartment, and save the rest of my paycheck to buy undeveloped real estate. I knew the local countryside well and assumed that numerous rural parcels were out there for the asking at tax-sale prices.

Unfortunately, as one might expect from a communications major, I gave little thought to the financial details. Such as how much I could realistically save in a year and whether or not any bank would lend me money to buy undeveloped land that I didn't plan to develop (as it turned out, they would not). After five years, I'd bought one piece of property, a landlocked, three-acre woods that can only be reached by canoe.

By the mid-1990s, I was ready to get married and needed to save money for a house. But I hadn't lost my urge to save wild places. And, since doing something was better than nothing, I decided to join the Nature Conservancy.

In all the world, there's no environmental organization like the Nature Conservancy. It's a conservation powerhouse that has protected 15 million acres in the United States and another 102 million in twenty-seven countries worldwide. In return for my membership dues, they sent a static window sticker and a gorgeous, bimonthly magazine that profiled the Nature Conservancy's preserves. My

favorite section was the roundup column in back, which lists all the new acreage they've protected since the last issue. It gave me a vicarious thrill to think that my twenty-five-dollar donation had been part of that.

Gradually, however, my enthusiasm began to wane. I noticed that the organization never, ever protected land near my home in southern Michigan. As I learned more about the Nature Conservancy, the reason became clear. The Nature Conservancy looks for pristine lands that harbor threatened species. It seeks to protect those "last great places," whose ecosystems—wild beaches, forests, marshes, and prairies—contain the best of what's left to save.

It's a logical approach and one that's rooted in sound science and field research. I've visited several Nature Conservancy preserves and have high praise for what the organization has achieved. All the same, this much seems true: by the Nature Conservancy's standards, there is no land in St. Joseph County worthy of protection.

Then, quite by accident while at an Earth Day celebration in nearby Kalamazoo, I came across an organization that did care about the wild places I cared about.

"Hey Tom—Tom Springer," called a bearded stranger from behind a makeshift booth. "I saw your article in the *Kalamazoo Gazette*."

A few weeks earlier I'd written a guest-rant editorial on suburban sprawl for the local paper. He must have recognized me from the mug shot that ran with the story.

"You should join our group, the River Country Conservancy," he said. "It's a new land trust, and we could really use more members."

At that point, my self-funded land trust had saved three acres, while these upstarts had yet to rescue a single acorn. But how could I refuse a personal invitation to finally do something useful on behalf of local conservation? Maybe it was time for the Lone Green Crusader to hang up his tights.

I didn't know it then, but I'd just been swept up by a grassroots social phenomenon: the land trust movement. For two decades, land trusts have grown at a remarkable rate. By 2003, there were fifteen hundred of them, a number that's more than doubled since 1990. In total, they protect 9.3 million acres—more than double the acreage they protected in 1998.

Land trusts protect land in a very direct manner. They raise money to buy property outright, accept gifts of donated land, or enter into a binding legal agreement with a landowner that's known as a conservation easement.

Under a conservation easement, the landowner agrees to place a deed restriction on his or her property to prevent the land from being developed. The easement usually results in substantial tax breaks for the landowner since the potential for development has been removed. In exchange, the rest of us get what's known as "public value" through the environmental benefits and tranquil scenery that wild places provide. The conservation easement will stay in place "in perpetuity," even when the land changes ownership.

Land trusts have been around since the nineteenth century, but they didn't become well established until the 1950s and 1960s when the environmental movement took hold. Understandably, land trusts are most numerous near fast-growing cities. It's there, faced with runaway development, that citizens are most eager to protect what's left. As Winston Churchill said, "Americans will always do the right thing . . . after they've exhausted all the alternatives."

It's also there, on the suburban fringe, that Americans confront their long-standing ambivalence about growth. Managing this ambivalence can be one of the most challenging aspects of a land trust's work.

On one hand, the notion of an ever-expanding city is a cherished American ideal. Endless growth is a central tenet of our capitalistic ideology, the engine that drives what Edward Abbey called "our crackpot expand or expire economy." How often do we elect public officials who say they're *against* growth? Growth means more jobs and more affluence for everyone. Growth means more stuff and more beige vinyl-sided storage units where people can stash all the stuff that no longer fits into their houses because (what else?) they've outgrown them.

Yet growth also collides, quite literally, with another enduring American ideal: our love of wilderness and pastoral working landscapes such as farms and ranches—the seedbed from which our pioneer nation sprung. It's ingrained in our social DNA, this yearning to rest in the bosom of wild America. Who doesn't long for a cozy cabin in the woods somewhere?

But here's the paradox: despite our quest for endless growth, we've long felt disquieted by the paradise we've despoiled along the way. It's that sense of loss that the poet Stephen Vincent Benet must have had in mind when he wrote those haunting lines that schoolkids of my generation once knew by heart.

When Daniel Boone goes by, at night
The phantom deer arise,
And all lost, wild America
is burning in their eyes.

In a more practical vein, as early as 1859, Henry David Thoreau argued that each town should set aside a nature preserve where not "a stick is cut for firewood." He urged the protection of small meadows, individual rock formations, and "and ancient trees standing singly" that give places their natural character.

"If the inhabitants of a town were wise," Thoreau wrote, "they would seek to preserve these things . . . for they educate far more than any hired teachers or preachers, or any present system of school education."

Another New England dreamer, Robert Frost, voiced similar themes in his work. In 1921, when suburbs were still a novelty, Frost wrote presciently of a growing town that destroys a wild stream in his poem "A Brook in the City."

The brook was thrown deep in a sewer dungeon under stone
In fetid darkness still to live and run—
And all for nothing it had ever done,
Except forget to go in fear perhaps.
No one would know except for ancient maps
That such a brook ran water. But I wonder
If from its being kept forever under,
The thoughts may not have risen that so keep
This new-built city from both work and sleep.

Instead of simply bemoaning the demise of nature, land trusts allow ordinary people to help prevent it. What's made land trusts so popular is that their mission is unabashedly local. They don't worry much about Chinese panda bears or lost tribes in the Amazon. Land trust members focus their energy on a remnant tall grass prairie or a little brook that's about to disappear "in a sewer dungeon under stone" (more likely a steel culvert these days). And they're eager to save a twenty-acre chunk of woods that borders a subdivision even if it's not home to an endangered species poster child.

Equally important, land trusts allow people to commit their bodies and souls to the good work of conservation. At a land trust preserve, there are trails to build and wild seeds to sow and gather. There's always brush to cut and haul and always some Godzilla-strength invasive plant that must be pulled or poisoned before its strangles some native species into oblivion. It's tough love, and land trusts serve it to their members in spades because without unpaid grunt labor they couldn't afford to maintain their properties.

And that's as it should be. For you can't really know a place until its driven thorns beneath your fingernails, inflamed your private parts with poison ivy, or singed your eyebrows during a "controlled" prairie burn. By contrast, the only physical activity that most big environmental groups ask of you—and ask they do with annoying frequency—is to stuff a personal check into one of their self-addressed envelopes.

With all that's going for them, land trusts seem to be the ideal organization for an average person who's passionate about local conservation. And that's true. I've been involved with a land trust for more than twelve years, and it's been one of my life's most rewarding experiences. We've found no shortage of altruistic people who want to save land along with a surprising number who have donated generous sums of money.

What we didn't see growing among us, however, were the seeds of a conflict that nearly tore us apart.

When I first joined the land trust, I expected some conflict, though of a different variety. Demographically, I didn't feel like an environmentalist. I was a centrist Republican, a regular churchgoer, and a staff sergeant in the National Guard who loves to catch fish and eat venison. I owned no hemp clothing, had no Swedish furniture, and, as a former UAW factory worker, still couldn't bring myself to buy a Japanese-made car.

But in short order I learned that none of this mattered. Land trusts, by there very nature, are apolitical. They rarely take stands on hot-button environmental issues, preferring instead to work quietly with local landowners to save land. Like others who are exasperated by partisan politics, I find this approach most appealing. It allows land trusts to attract people of goodwill from across the political spectrum.

This bipartisan spirit has enlivened our organization in surprising ways. For instance, at our famous potlucks, it's usually the leftists who bring the best whole grain breads, elderberry pies, lentil soups, and organic, God knows what salsa. Which is all for the good. Because right wingers, otherwise adept at running the universe, are often culinary dullards whose idea of picnic cuisine is to drown a bag of lethally salty finger sausages in a Crock-Pot of Wal-Mart's Own barbecue sauce.

So, to paraphrase Saint Paul, "If liberals and conservatives be for us, then who be against us?" If only it were that easy. For the fatal flaws that bedeviled us were those that all mortals share: pride, stubbornness, and the maddening human tendency to resist change.

In a perverse way, the problem was a by-product of the organization's success. As mentioned earlier, the land trust was first run by volunteers. After a few years, we were able to hire an executive director and part-time secretary. Even so, the volunteers still did an enormous amount of work. We raised money, met with potential land donors, scouted new properties, painted the office, donated furniture, and offered free legal and financial advice. Although we weren't paid, the intrinsic benefits were huge. To protect land is a deeply rewarding undertaking. It's a job many of us would kill to have (even if we got Cs in biology) because it benefits the world in such a tangible, useful way.

At first, volunteers pitched in because they had to. Yet our stated goal was to save more land and do it more effectively. To do that, we needed to hire more professionals—which we did. After ten years, the organization had a full-time staff of five capable people. But as the staff grew it became harder and harder for the old guard volunteers to let go. We still wanted to be Lone Green Crusaders. We wanted to decide which land to protect, how preserves should be managed, or, in my case, how to write the newsletter. Regardless of the issue, it really came down to one question. How much of our egos and control were we willing to cede for the greater good of the organization?

The ongoing conflict was making life miserable for the staff and the executive director. As things came to a head, it was time for a Come to Jesus meeting—otherwise known as a strategic planning session. It was held at the country estate of a volunteer (likely a Republican given the startling number of very un-Democratic wild game mounts that adorned his living room). What came out of that long, often painful meeting was a workable solution. Basically, we'd stop acting like a hobby club and more like a well-run, nonprofit organization. We would become a governing board of directors, one that set policies, approved purchases, and set guidelines for the executive director. Volunteers would still do much hands-on work but under the guidance of a full-time staff.

As for the executive director, he'd be accountable to the board but would manage the organization as he saw fit, and we would refrain from meddling in his daily affairs. Ideally, our organization would become a community of diverse people who would submerge their personal agendas to save land for the greater good. In effect, we'd exemplify what we expected other people and communities to do.

It wasn't easy, but we eventually overcame our growing pains, although some good volunteers chose to leave. And, like parents watching their kids fly the nest, it's been both gratifying and melancholic to see the transformation take place. Our homegrown land trust has saved six thousand acres and continues to add another thousand acres per year. But gone are the maverick days when I could deputize myself to cut dead trees for firewood at a preserve. There are management plans in place for that sort of thing now.

What we still have, however, is a welcome attitude toward anyone who shares our cause. To me, that means as much as anything we've accomplished. For if war is too important to be left to generals then conservation is too important to be left to self-proclaimed environmentalists. There's even room for developers in silky golf shirts—and we've met a few—who are willing to set aside wild lands to create nature preserves.

What sums it up best is a heartening encounter that occurred during a springtime workday at one of our preserves. We were there to cut glossy buckthorn and Japanese honeysuckle, followed by a walking tour with a naturalist. There among the crowd I spotted a high school classmate (I'll call him Randy) who I hadn't seen in twenty-five years.

After high school, Randy studied applied forestry at a trade school in Kentucky, and he's been a logger ever since. He spends his days in the Michigan woods, marking trees and felling them for harvest. Yet in recent years Randy has realized how much he loves trees, and that's made him much more conservation minded.

"There are some bad actors in this business, but I practice responsible forestry," he said. "I don't clear-cut. I take out the diseased and crooked trees that other guys leave behind. And I don't tear up the woods and make it a bramble patch."

Mind you, he said this at a gathering of tree huggers, knowing full well that in some environmental circles he'd be denounced as the devil incarnate. Or even have his tires slashed. It took courage for Randy the logger to be there that day, and that's why his next comment really hit home.

After we'd talked awhile, he asked with some hesitation, "So uh, what kind of group is this anyway?"

I could have given him the usual, "Well, Randy, a land trust is a 501 (c) 3 nonprofit organization that blah, blah, blah . . ." But I could tell he wasn't looking for that. He just wanted to know if this was a place where he'd feel welcome. Where people would treat him as a person first and perhaps even value his great love and knowledge of trees.

So I explained that we weren't a political organization. I said we had members who hunt and fish, as well as card-carrying vegetarians who never do anything more violent than pull garlic mustard and dandelions. Randy liked that explanation and has since become a member. When I left that day, he was having a friendly debate with a bushy-bearded leftist about whether a certain tree was a basswood or a slippery elm.

For the record, this little drama took place at a preserve that's too small and unremarkable for any big organization or government agency to bother with. But we're fine with that. We know it as a pocket wilderness, where cardinal flowers and wild iris bloom in the rich soil of a floodplain forest. Maybe it's not one of the world's last great places, but it's our place, and it's our land trust. And if we want to save the world our own neighborhood seems like a good place to start.

IN NATURE, THE STRAIGHT LINE
LEADS TO PERDITION

The best piece of advice I ever heard about landscaping comes from a man who was not a landscaper.

"The straight line belongs to man," said Antoni Gaudí, "and the curve to God."

Gaudí (1852–1926), was a Spanish architect who designed Barcelona's bizarre and beautiful Church of the Holy Family (Sagrada Familia). Its organic design reminds me of my kids' Lake Michigan sand castles, whose lumpy parapets are decorated with whatever stones, shells, and crayfish carcasses we find at hand. The art critic Jonathan Glancey described the Sagrada Familia—which is still unfinished—as a "tall bed of stone vegetation" unlike any other in the world. Of Gaudí's work in general, Glancey said it expresses a "weird geometry" that "connects humans both to God and nature."

For Gaudí, it seems that being too straight was a violation of the natural order (a belief that would no doubt get him banned from the *700 Club*). Yet, as someone who's seen the errors of right-angled thinking, I believe Gaudí was correct. In thought and deed, we humans are always eager to impose our straightness on creation. We assume that a direct line is the best route between two points—although the hand of nature usually chooses otherwise.

A good way to see the flaws of linear thinking is to plan your own landscape project. My first such endeavor, after we bought our farmhouse, was to establish a boundary of wild habitat between ourselves and the farm field next door. For starters, I bought a truckload of

three-foot white pines that were on sale at a local nursery. I didn't bother to draw up a plan. Had I done so, it probably would have had a lot of little squares on it.

Our four-acre parcel is rectangular. So, in deference to the unyielding authority of the survey stakes, I planted the trees in the most unimaginative way possible: *exactly* fifty feet apart, in a single-file row, ker-plop, ker-plop, ker-plop. Needless to say, I used a tape measure.

The next spring brought unusually dry weather, and the young trees needed water at least once a week. To make the job easier, I mowed a path alongside them. It would also double as a "nature trail" that would encircle the property. To me, it looked great. The freshly mowed walkway was as straight as a Utah Republican's voting record. My perpendicular logic was imposing order on the chaos of an overgrown soybean field.

Then a friendly neighbor—as only friends can do—gleefully pointed out the inanity of my rigid approach to "natural" landscaping.

"Hey, Tom, you got those trees planted real straight!" he said. "That must be how they grow in the forest, huh?"

I was out in the field, shovel in hand, sweating bullets in a deerfly free-fire zone. He was leisurely riding past on his bike, and his laughter echoed jeeringly down the ramrod row of little trees.

My sister-in-law—as only family members can be—was even more direct.

"Jeez, Tom, what did you mow such a straight path for? It's so bor-r-r-ing. A good trail needs to have some surprises along the way. You need some curves and bends; some visual interest."

Visual interest? That made me a little huffy. After all, I fancied myself the family's environmental expert. Who was she, the queen of Round-Up and MiracleGro, to enlighten me about green landscaping? Here I was, raring to create the township's first restored prairie and maybe even raise organic musk ox. How could anyone accuse me, Mr. Whole Grain, of white-bread thinking?

A behavioral psychologist might say that I'd been conditioned to think this way. Like a fish in a rectangular tank, I was raised in a square house surrounded by a grid of streets and sidewalks. At school, I sat at a square desk and read square books all day. During army basic training, my drill sergeant spent twelve weeks marching our platoon all over Fort Knox, a moving box of straight-jawed soldiers that turned only in ninety-degree directions. Now that I'm an adult, need I mention the shape of the car, office cubicle, and computer screen that delineate the boundaries of my waking hours?

For some of us, such as my wife Nancy, this conditioning has been less successful. She readily sees how the fluid designs of nature can bring variety to a man-made landscape. For instance, when we bought our farmhouse there were no real flowerbeds—just a narrow row of sedums that bordered the fieldstone foundation. When it came time to enlarge the beds, Nancy didn't ask my opinion on how to do it. Had she done so, I probably would have said "Well, Nance, why not bring 'em straight out from the house another foot? Let me run and get my tape measure and edging spade" (the one with a nice square tip)!

Instead, Nancy did something that to me was unfathomable. She went to a garden store and had them sketch out a basic landscape plan with nary a straight line on it. The guy did it for free on tracing paper in number 2 pencil, but it served the purpose. Gradually, as time and money allowed, the plan has taken shape. I first suspect there's a new project afoot when Nancy lays out her black garden hose in the form of a new bed. As if re-creating a garden-party crime scene, she traces its outline on the turf in white spray paint. Within a few weeks, another patch of scruffy grass has been transformed into a kidney- or scallop-shaped planting that softens the angular borders of our home.

As for me, although good advice is the hardest kind to take, I've learned that my wife and sister-in-law are on to something. For starters, I mowed gentle bends and loops into the trails. The field is still square, but to anyone who walks the paths its character has changed into something less rigid and predictable. The trail has become more than a lawn-tractor service road. The curves and nodes create focal points, places where the eye and spirit can linger to behold a wildflower or fresh clump of coyote scat.

Of course, for even amateur landscapers this is basic stuff. You don't need Antoni Gaudí's appreciation for "weird geometry" to figure it out. Most gardening magazines include basic blueprints that will transform your cubist yard into a refuge of winding walkways and peninsulas of perennials that are anything but square.

For me, the bigger change came as I began to apply this circular logic to my role as the property's caretaker. Maybe I couldn't control the overall shape of my property. But within its boundaries, I could yield more to the curvaceous caprice of nature than to the one-way reasoning of mechanized humanity. Instead of making nature conform to my own yardstick, I could try to find my rightful place in the life cycle.

A case in point has been my plan to establish a half-acre patch of prairie and savanna just east of our house. By definition, a prairie consists almost entirely of grass, shrubs, and wildflowers. A savanna, known as an "oak opening" in southern Michigan, is like a prairie with trees. The trees—usually burr or black oak—cover from 10 to 80 percent of the surface area. Most people think of primeval Michigan as heavily forested. But in much of southern Michigan prairies and savannas were predominant.

I've always been fascinated by this landscape and pioneer accounts of its beauty and fertility. Even in its virginal state, the oak savanna must have seemed wild yet welcoming, a habitable compromise between the dark vastness of a forest and the naked vulnerability of a treeless plain. There were enough trees for shade and timber but enough open grassland to encourage agriculture.

Perhaps it's this appeal that attracted my great-great-grandfather, Noah Springer, to move here from Bucks County, Pennsylvania, in 1854. After traveling by covered wagon, he settled a few miles away on Prairie Ronde. Nearly ten miles long and five miles wide, it was the largest piece of native grassland in Southwest Michigan.

Because of farmers such as Noah, many new plants began to grow on the prairie. Not just cash crops such as corn and wheat but European weed species such as Queen Anne's lace, common mullein, and chicory. They hitchhiked in, I suppose, in the pockets, wagon wheels, and feed bags of pioneers. Within a few years, these newcomers were well established both in cultivated fields and in forests and wetlands. They were as rooted in the local ecosystem as the burr oaks and buffalo used to be.

My patch of prairie bears clear evidence of this history. Even after decades of heavy grazing and row-crop agriculture, it's home to natives such as lead plant, butterfly weed, and big bluestem. Growing among them is a melting pot of European and Asian immigrants that seem happy to call Michigan their home. For better or worse, what grows there is a new rendition of the prairie with an adapted ecology all its own.

Ah, but here's the irony. If I'm to create a real prairie, then all this has to go. In so many words, I've been told by prairie restoration experts that I'll need to destroy my existing prairie in order to save it.

And from a technical standpoint they are exactly right. If you want a historically correct prairie, a piece of tall-grass heaven just like the one that Laura Ingalls Wilder wrote about, then you'll need to do plenty of killing and tilling. You must first spray herbicide, extermi-

nate every living plant, and then till under the dead remains. You should then repeat this kill-and-till cycle for one or two growing seasons, as necessary, until every fugitive seed and shoot has shriveled into submission. Only after Mother Earth cries "uncle" is it safe to plant your all natural prairie.

Again, from the standpoint of efficiency, this is indeed the best way to go. If you're converting a large piece of land into prairie, the shortest distance between two points is to fire up the tractor, fill up the spray rig, and plow a straight furrow back to the nineteenth century. Prairie plants and seeds are very expensive. To become established, they need as little competition as possible from weeds and nonnative grasses.

Yet on my half-acre prairie I've decided to forgo this conventional shock-and-awe approach. For one thing, it requires far too much work for something that's supposed to be a hobby. The larger objection, however, has to do with my respect for what's already there. It goes back to circular thinking and my place in the larger picture. Who am I to destroy my truly native plants—ecotypes whose ancestors may date to the ice age—and replace them with "native" specimens that were raised in a nursery?

As for the exotics, while I'm less fond of them, some may have been here for 170 years (much longer than my human kin). We know that plants communicate via chemical means, and maybe they've found a symbiotic way to coexist with the natives. They may even provide benefits that we've yet to understand. So at what point do these naturalized foreigners earn their botanical green card?

My unscientific restoration method allows me to enrich instead of eradicate. In practice, that means I buy flats of native grasses and wildflowers and plant them as randomly as possible on the little prairie. After a few weeks of initial watering, they're on their own. It's a tough-love approach, but life on a prairie isn't for the weak or wilt prone. This is the twenty-first century, and if the natives can't hack it then their ecological duties may be outsourced to some hardy honeysuckle bush from western Ukraine.

As much I'd love to see a ten-thousand-acre native prairie, I know that Prairie Ronde is gone forever. All that I can do is help sustain the world that I've inherited. Given ample time and space, I'm confident that something good will come of it. Nature is infinitely creative and adaptive. It will find ways to fit even the most aggressive exotic species—zebra mussels, purple loosestrife, kudzu—into a cohesive new whole. Without this resilience, our world wouldn't have lasted for five billion years.

Whether the bit players in this landscape drama are native or foreign, the performance is always enjoyable. On this mid-October day, as I take a writing break to tour the prairie, clumps of little bluestem shimmer in the sun like fountains of molten copper. The Queen Anne's lace flower heads have turned brown and are curled into little baskets that resemble a hummingbird's nest. On the prickly pear cactus, I see several pink fruits about to ripen. Maybe this year I'll summon enough courage to eat one.

On my way back in, I take a beeline detour to the mailbox. I'm preoccupied, as insecure writers often are, about what correspondence awaits me there. As I cross the road, I'm jarred into attentiveness by the rumble of a semitruck loaded with field corn. I've just been reading about Gaudí and realize that unless I wake up I could damn well end up like him. Which is to say dead in a most absurd and tragic fashion.

Gaudí was a shy, pious man who never married. In his later years, he lived a monklike existence in the crypt of his beloved Sagrada Familia. One day, to get a better look at the church's incomplete tower, he stepped into the busy street. Soon after, a tram came barreling along and struck the white-bearded architect. Because of his worn clothing, he was taken for a beggar and died a few days later in a hospital for the poor.

Gaudí is a national hero to many Spaniards, and there have been attempts to have him canonized a saint. All that's lacking are a few miracles on his behalf.

Well, anyone who designs apartment complexes with facades that look like scaly lizards and balconies like mythic beasts would certainly get my vote. He'd be no plaster saint, either. Just a humble guy whose gift was to shape stone and steel into buildings that resonate with the holy energy of an ancient tree or mountain.

So here's to you, Antoni Gaudí, would-be patron of free-form gardeners and earth-loving architects. With your help, may the paths we trod always follow a delightfully crooked way.

TICKED OFF BY GUINEAS

Many people who move to the country are smitten by an urge to surround themselves with a menagerie of farm animals. I am not in that camp. There is enough daily maintenance required by the one dog, two cats, and two free-range children that share our 1860s vintage home (which itself is in perpetual need of maintenance).

As a hobby, I've found it more leisurely to care for trees, flowerbeds, and vegetable gardens. For one thing, they tend to stay put and make very little noise. Of all the trees I've planted, not one has had to be nursed, inoculated, sheared, milked, butchered, or chased around the countryside on a cold and rainy night. So for several years we lived on an un-animal farm and were proud of it.

That all changed on a June morning a few years ago when my wife was called at work by a distraught nursery school teacher.

"Mrs. Springer?" she said. "We just pulled what looks like a tick from inside your daughter's ear."

The proper reaction—when told that your child is afflicted with vermin—should be one of surprise and concern. While my wife's concern was genuine, her surprise was a bit feigned. We had known for some time that our property was teeming with ticks.

In fact, the tick problem had reached creepy proportions well before the nursery school incident. It wasn't enough that I pulled blood-engorged ticks from the dog that were often the size of a grape. The ticks also had my number. After an evening's work in the fencerow, I once picked sixteen of the hitch hikers from my skin and clothing.

And picture this. You're at work, where you've just begun a long meeting in a wood-paneled office. Suddenly, reacting to a strange sensation near your collar, you discover that a bloodthirsty parasite has affixed itself to your neck. You pull it off, real sneaky like, then sit nonchalantly with a tick clenched between your thumbnail and forefinger. What exactly is the proper business etiquette for disposing of that?

As a point of clarification, since these were dog ticks, they didn't pose a serious health risk. It is deer ticks, not dog ticks, that carry the debilitating Lyme disease. It takes a dog tick about twenty-four hours to begin drawing blood. If removed sooner than that, there's little chance of harm. Even so, it was time for us to do *something*. Otherwise, the next phone call might be from a caseworker at the Department of Social Services.

The real culprit, we suspected, was the orchard grass that covers about half of our acreage. Orchard grass is a dense, nonnative perennial that reaches about twenty-four inches in height by midsummer. Ticks prefer tall grass since short grass gets too hot and dry for them to live in. The easiest, fastest way to kill ticks in tall grass is to spray them with commercial pesticide. Unfortunately, the pesticide doesn't care what else it kills. Along with ticks, it will indiscriminately kill birds, bees, butterflies, and other beneficial insects. For us, such collateral damage was unacceptable.

The other route was to use what our county extension agent called a biological control—a natural way to kill something that doesn't involve toxic substances. What we needed, several local sources assured me, were guinea hens. Guinea hens, they said, were veritable tick-eatin' machines. It was this organic approach that led us to plumb the untested waters of farm animal management. We bought six fuzzy guinea keets (chicks), which I carried home from the feed store in a shoe box.

Guineas are hardy foot soldiers of the fowl world, still able to roost in trees and nest on the ground like their wild ancestors. As a member of the Galliformes family, guinea fowl are a close relative of the turkey. Native to Africa, they were introduced to Europe in the fifteenth century and have been residents of North America since the early days of white settlement. Guinea flesh supposedly tastes like pheasant, and their edible eggs are similar to those of a chicken. Unlike chickens, free-range guineas aren't fussy about where they lay their eggs, which can make them difficult for people to find.

The sight and sound of a guinea is unmistakable. Their surprisingly loud, machine-gun squawk—and they love to squawk—resembles that of a peacock. A guinea has a head that's covered in leathery white skin complimented by red wattles. The skinny neck sits atop a body that's shaped like an army helmet. Still, in their own way guineas are attractive. The most common variety has pearl gray feathers covered with little white polka dots.

Along with their penchant for chemical-free pest control, what sold us on guineas was their low-maintenance reputation. There's a big difference, however, between low-maintenance and no maintenance.

Our guinea chicks' first home was a dog cage that I'd set up inside an old lean-to shed. They had ample food, water, and overhead shelter. But at this stage any young living creature is tragically vulnerable, and guineas are no exception. Only two of our brood reached maturity—coyotes and raccoons got the rest. In what grisly fashion they reached through the cage to seize their prey, I hate to imagine. Four of the fatalities occurred while we were away for the weekend. By the time the two survivors were big enough to run free, tick season had come and gone. During the next four months of winter, our snowbound freeloaders ate twenty-five pounds of laying mash.

Next spring the orchard grass grew tall and the ticks returned. Only guess what? Instead of roaming the tall grass, the guinea (we were down to one by then) rarely left the yard and driveway. She didn't have to. Everything a guinea gal could want was right there.

Guineas are omnivorous eaters and in their own way can be as indiscriminate as any pesticide. The two gooseberry bushes by the side door? Every last berry—gone. The low-hanging serviceberries from the prize tree in our side yard? Gulped and gone. For variety, in a shower of fresh dirt and mulch, the guinea would scratch through the tulip and annual beds around the front porch, eating, I'm sure, any "good insect" (honeybee, butterfly, praying mantis) that crossed her path.

Worst of all, she formed a bizarre, cross-species attachment to my Olds sedan. Perhaps loneliness drove her to it. We don't have a garage, so the guinea roosted on my car every night. Each morning, I'd sweep off a fresh clump of cigarette-sized droppings from the hood. As I drove away, the guinea would run alongside me for fifty yards or so, squawking her head off like a jilted lover.

Over time, her affections strayed. By August, any car that paused by the stop sign near our house was fair game for her advances. To say the least, we got many startled looks from drivers who wondered why a squawking, helmet-shaped bird was assaulting their door handles.

The guinea's illicit car fetish came to no good. Coming home from work one day, my brother found her sprawled flat in the intersection. He stuffed her into an empty grain sack to spare our kids from seeing the carnage. Thus ended our feathered campaign of organic pest control.

Nevertheless, when you try something that fails this stupendously, it is useful to ask: "What the hell was I thinking?" The six innocent guineas that expired due to my negligence certainly deserve that much.

For starters, rural amateurs often underestimate what it takes to raise plants and animals successfully. This is ironic because in other areas of our lives we place a premium on professional credentials and fact-based logic. Not so, however, with matters agricultural. We'd rather just plop it in the ground (or the barn) and naively trust in the good fairy of our green intentions.

This flawed thinking is often based on a worthy desire to do things "organically." For good reason, many people would rather not use man-made herbicides, pesticides, and animal growth hormones. But organic agriculture requires far more than letting nature take its course. The do next to nothing approach (in terms of weed and pest control) was first tried in the 1960s by a new breed of farmers who sought to raise their crops in a chemical-free fashion. In most cases, they failed miserably. For, as generals like to say, "Hope is not a method." And neither is benign neglect. You still need a way—conventional or organic—to keep the weeds and destructive bugs at bay.

Today, most organic farmers consider their approach more complex and labor intensive than conventional farming. Conventional farmers rely heavily on external expertise and technology, using chemical sprays and fertilizers that were developed in far-off laboratories. For organic farmers, observation and knowledge of local conditions are crucial. They strive to create a balanced ecosystem where soils are made fertile by adding organic matter and unwanted bugs are eaten by natural predators. Organic farmers spend more time walking, watching, and listening to the land. Early detection is crucial because organic sprays (made from substances such as hot peppers) don't have the knockout power of agrochemicals. It takes in-depth knowledge of plant and insect cycles to know where and when to use these less toxic methods.

On a much smaller scale, I've learned this the hard way. The dysfunctional guinea is the most recent of my failed attempts at chemical-free pest control. A few years ago, I tried using a shop vac to suck up a swarm of squash beetles that invaded our garden. It was great fun, but the pumpkins died anyway. Before that, I tried to stop deer from munching my trees by sprinkling them with hair clippings from my Dad's barbershop.

These techniques may sound ineffectual, but they were based on proven practices. What failed was the planning and execution. Organic farmers do use chickens to control insect pests in their fields and orchards—but they house the birds in rolling chicken coops. Organic farmers do use tractor-mounted vacuums to remove undesirable bugs from their strawberry plants—but they do so before the insects reach epidemic stage, as they did in my pumpkin patch. As for using human hair to scare away deer . . . well, that's what you get for listening to aged malingerers in a small-town barbershop.

Our specific problem, as you may recall, was ticks. And I'm proud to say that we finally reduced their number. We did it by using a modified biological control that millions of suburbanites pursue with religious zeal: it's called mowing. By extending the lawn one hundred feet beyond the swing set, we've been able to keep our kids nearly tick free. The dog and I still attract ticks in the tall grass, but the teacher doesn't need to know that.

For those Americans raised on canned peas, Jell-O salad, and Wonder Bread, the word *organic* will always have a certain wholesome appeal. And it's good to see the sale of organic products grow steadily each year. Yet, if you grow your own, don't expect natural controls to work unless you're willing to invest the time and research they require. Otherwise, you'll probably end up disillusioned—and maybe even with a psycho guinea hen for a hood ornament.

CARETAKERS AND CHARACTERS

STREETS, TREES, AND
A RARE ENGINEER WHO
LOVES THEM BOTH

It may not have been psychologically healthy, but for a time in 1968 my two best friends had bark on them. They were at least one hundred years old yet still sturdy with the vigor of youth. Each afternoon they'd wait faithfully by the sidewalk to greet me when I walked home from school. One of their roots stuck out like a knobby knee from the trunk. And on this woody throne I'd sit and ponder my recently reconfigured life.

In today's lingo, we would say that I was a fourth grader "who had issues." Specifically, I was angry about our move from a NASA bedroom community in Melbourne, Florida, to the family's ancestral home of Three Rivers, Michigan (population 7,800). Or, as I saw it, from the world capital of 1960s space age hipdom to a dull farm burg where neither the kids nor the adults could tell an Apollo capsule from a corncrib.

"Where they a goin' this time, to Mars?" asked a middle-aged woman in Three Rivers when we tried to tell her about the upcoming moon mission. I hadn't known that grown-ups were allowed to be so ignorant of world affairs.

While my parents were native Michiganders, I'd spent most of my nine years in Florida. That was home to me, and I especially missed the ocean. I longed for the wild beaches of Cape Canaveral; I hungered for the jumbo shrimp and blue crab that my Dad and I would net from the city pier by the glow of a Coleman lantern.

What I didn't know was that Michigan's allure has a way of sneaking up on you.

We arrived in late summer, and with the Detroit Tigers fighting for the pennant I at first paid little attention to the trees of Three Rivers. Had you asked, I might have said they were old, gray, and boring—much like the town's buildings, schools, and teachers for that matter.

Then one Indian summer afternoon, as I walked home from school, I was struck full force by the unexpected beauty of our new home. The streets in my neighborhood were lined with old sugar maples. And overhead, as the sun burst forth from a patch of indigo sky, the trees seemed to distill the very essence of autumn. As if lit from within, their gold and orange foliage glowed with a heavenly luminosity. It was a midwestern autumn in all its glory, and I'd never seen anything like it.

For a few magic weeks afterward, the leaves were everywhere: adorning the trees, rustling underfoot, burning in sweet windrows along the curbs, twirling down in cyclones of brilliant orange and yellow to cover the lawns and streets. I missed Florida less and less after that. The trees, and a new school friend, had made me feel much more welcome.

Nearly forty years later that same maple still stands outside my grandmother's former home. But every year more and more of its companions are cut down. And what they're replaced with is rarely a sugar maple. In fact, whoever's in charge of planting street trees seems bent on planting as many varieties as possible. With each new tree, the town loses more of the visual harmony that a street lined with beautiful trees of a similar shape, size, and species can provide.

This is, admittedly, a pet peeve that many would find extremely petty. Far bigger concerns face Three Rivers, including the steady loss of manufacturing jobs and a new Wal-Mart that is threatening to snuff out a recent renaissance in the downtown district. Yet we are who we are, and the demise of the town's sugar maples is a problem that I can easily get my mind (and even arms) around.

For several years, I ranted about this situation to anyone who listened. As is often the case with pet peeves, I never bothered to get my facts straight. Since I didn't bother to find the answer, the answer eventually had to find me.

My enlightenment came during a chance encounter with an un-

likely tutor, E. Merritt Brown, special projects engineer for the city of Three Rivers. Merritt and I met when we paddled down the Rocky River (one of the town's three rivers) on a trip sponsored by the St. Joseph County Conservation District. While our outing was a short one, I had brought along plenty of personal baggage—and not of the recreational variety.

The reason I saw Merritt as an unlikely tutor is that, in my experience, the public servants who build and maintain roads often show great hostility toward trees. It's as if trees, by their very existence, threaten the man-made dominion of asphalt and the motoring republic for which its stands. On many American road projects, majestic trees are bulldozed into smoldering heaps when they pose only the remotest threat to passing traffic. The few that remain are often trimmed so severely that they never regain their natural vigor.

For me, there's no better example of this institutional bias than the boom mower used by road crews in St. Joseph County to "trim" roadside trees. A boom mower consists of a tractor with a long, jointed arm that's attached to a heavy-duty mower deck. It's designed to cut grass and brush in hard-to-reach places such as on hillsides or along the back side of a fence. But when used to "trim" trees the boom mower operates with all the finesse of a Civil War era field surgeon.

Once extended into a tree's canopy, the boom mower functions like a huge weed whacker. It leaves in its wake a grisly harvest of splintered limbs, shattered branches, and strips of shredded bark that hang from the trees like malevolent Christmas ornaments. Apart from being butt ugly, the jagged wounds make the trees more vulnerable to insect pests and disease.

If trimmed properly with a saw, a ring of new bark would form to enclose the spot where the limb was cut. Instead, the trauma inflicted by the boom mower makes the trees go haywire. They sprout an unhealthy array of scrawny shoots and weak branches, which, alas, only necessitates more boom mowing. The federal guidelines of the Environmental Protection Agency, which describe this condition as a "hurricane-aftermath look," stridently oppose the use of boom mowers in this fashion. It's infuriating that my county should follow such a crude, ghastly practice, especially since we promote our scenic country roads as a way to attract more tourists.

So the specter of boom mowers loomed large when I first met Merritt Brown, as did the fate of Three Rivers' aging sugar maples. Yet as we eased down the river in kayaks it became clear that Merritt's interests extended far beyond the hard-surface domain of streets, sidewalks, and public utilities. On his own initiative, he's taken on a secondary job as the city forester. He's become an engineer who plants trees, tends trees, loves trees, and knows far more about them than most of us ever will.

Merritt's a big man, built like a tight end, one of those guys who will probably be fit and strong well into his seventies. He's got a deep, senatorial voice and exudes a patient authority that sometimes hints at weariness. You suspect that he's spent much of his career around people who have far less mental candlepower then he does. Make an ill-informed assumption around him and he's quick to set the record straight.

"Well, let me ask you something, Merritt," I said, easing into a pseudo question that I saw more as a statement of fact. "The city cuts down a lot of old sugar maples, but how come they never replace them with sugar maples? They've got so much more character than the Bradford pears, crab apples, and other spindly stuff they put in these days."

"Well, Tom, I'm with you on that," Merritt boomed cheerily. "I love sugar maples and wish I could plant more of them. It looks great to see a street that's lined with shade trees of a single size and species. But what's crucial with urban trees now is diversity."

With that, Merritt proceeded to dismantle the flawed foundation of my argument.

As he explained it, until the 1930s and 1940s, the predominant street tree in America was the American elm. Their towering trunks and graceful, vaselike form made them hugely popular. American elms lent the same classic character to small towns and cities that sugar maples have brought to Three Rivers. But the onset of Dutch elm disease changed that forever. In town after town, as the disease swept uncontrolled across the nation, entire streets and neighborhoods were left devoid of shade.

Unfortunately, with the increase of global trade, Dutch elm disease was only the beginning. New foreign pests now appear with frightful regularity, most recently the emerald ash borer. This tiny green insect has now killed or threatens to kill ash trees in towns and forests across America. The sad irony is that millions of these trees were planted as replacements for the American elm.

"So now we know better," Merritt said. "We don't know what the next exotic pest will be, but what we can do is plant a variety of trees. That way one disease can't wipe out everything."

Well, yes, of course.

The float trip ended with a customary beer and buffalo burger at

Brewster's, a riverside restaurant in Three Rivers that has a dock for its paddling customers. But what Merritt said about street trees led me to do some long overdue research.

Apart from aesthetics, I've learned that a strong argument can be made for street trees on practical grounds alone. In summer, the shade of a mature tree on a roof or wall can reduce surface temperatures by up to forty degrees Fahrenheit. In winter, a shelterbelt of trees, especially in open places, can greatly reduce the amount of heat lost due to wind exposure. Overhead, street trees soften the noise, dust, and glare of urban life.

What most intrigued me, however, was the unsung contribution that street trees make to the social fabric of a community. Mature street trees create what landscape architects refer to as "an outdoor room." They provide a leafy transition zone from the public street to the private realms of homes and gardens. This effect is especially pronounced in places such as Three Rivers, which was laid out on a rectangular grid of streets.

With the grid pattern, residential streets run parallel to a terrace of lawn that's dotted with evenly spaced shade trees. Beyond the terrace lies a sidewalk, and on many homes what overlooks the sidewalk is a broad front porch. It's a highly civilized design, one that safely accommodates vehicles and pedestrians. It's an arrangement that makes social contact easy and comfortable. Compare this to most modern suburbs, which have no sidewalks, no usable front porches, and three-car connected garages that allow occupants to enter and exit their homes—in fugitive fashion—without seeing another soul.

I was raised in a two-story house on West Bennett Street, where I still spend many summer evenings on my parents' front porch. When we're out there, it's rare that a person will walk by and not at least say hello. As habitual porch sitters, my parents have made friends with many folks (and their dogs, whom my father bribes with pet treats) that they wouldn't otherwise have met. In part, I attribute this civility to a streetscape that makes people more accessible and accountable to their neighbors. I also believe some credit must go to the trees and the peaceable attitudes they engender. But, like most everyday blessings, we appreciate them most after they're gone.

At the end of my parents' drive, the woman next door decided to cut down a big maple in her front yard. It was still fairly healthy and might have lived another fifty years, but a commercial tree trimmer conned her into it. Now, in the hole left by the tree's absence, the July sun roasts her house from late morning to late afternoon. Gone, too, is the soothing rustle of leaves outside her second-story bedroom window on a midsummer night. Does she regret her impulsiveness? I've never asked. But in the eighty years it will take to grow a replacement there'll be plenty of time to ponder the wisdom of her decision.

Nearly two years had passed since our float trip, but my fascination with urban forestry continued. The idea of an unseen hand behind it all intrigued me. So, with the stated intent of writing a profile for the local newspaper, I asked Merritt to meet me for breakfast at a local coffee joint.

"Well, Tom, you must not come here often," he said upon my arrival. "I saw you looking on the wrong side of the door for the handle!"

Same old Merritt. Before I could even sit down, he had to set me straight. My incompetence thus confirmed, we both ordered raisin toast and orange juice, which Merritt insisted on paying for.

As we began to talk, a few things became clear. First, there was no way I could write a newspaper article about the guy. I'm far too passionate about trees to cover the subject in an objective fashion.

More than that, my premise was all wrong. I'd seen this as a man bites dog story about the rare road builder who loves trees. In fact, it's his engineering knowledge that helps make Merritt a good urban forester. It gives him a huge advantage. He knows where all the sewer, water, gas, and electric lines are buried. He knows the required clearances for overhead utilities. He knows what happens to streets and sidewalks when the wrong trees are planted in the wrong places.

It makes you wonder if there isn't hope for other highwaymen as well. With a little green reeducation, who knows? Maybe even a boom mower jockey could come to appreciate chlorophyll as much as concrete.

Over the next hour, Merritt shared his personal history and professional philosophy. The quick version is that he grew up near Petoskey and learned to love the big beeches and maples that grew on his family's farm. When he enrolled at Michigan Technological University in Houghton, he intended to major in forestry. When that program was discontinued, he decided to earn a degree in civil engineering.

Among his achievements in Three Rivers, Merritt has drafted the city's first forestry code. It spells out the how, what, why, and where of the city's tree-planting and maintenance program. I haven't seen it, but after listening to Merritt I'm quite sure that it covers every conceivable detail down to the molecular level.

"We need *diversity,*" he reminded me, thumping his muskmelon fist on the table. "When I ask bidders to supply trees, I tell them no more than 5 percent of any species . . . no more than 15 percent of any genus. . . . Lately I've planted *Quercus palustrus* [pin oak]. . . . Oh, and a real nice zelkova. . . . They're tall, like an American elm, and . . ."

Class was in session, and Professor Merritt was clearly at home on the podium: "I won't take out a tree unless it's more than 50 percent dead. . . . We always plant trees on fifteen- to twenty-foot centers or they'll overcompete for sun and nutrients. . . . For traffic visibility and ground clearance, all trees need five feet to the first set of branches."

Then, as he continued talking, an unusual thing happened. People started to listen. And not just the usual eavesdropping you expect in a small-town coffee shop. They really listened. One fellow even asked permission to sit closer so he wouldn't miss anything.

"The first street trees in Three Rivers were planted in the late 1800s," Merritt explained, "at the end of the Victorian era when naturalism was very popular—people wanted to bring nature into the city. . . . The Prutzmans, the Hoffmans, the town's early families, they probably transplanted the maples from the countryside."

It seemed as if no one in the coffee shop had heard this before. They lived here, they knew Prutzman Street and Hoffman Street, but they didn't know their own history. You could see their interest and enthusiasm at being told about it for the first time.

Warming to his audience, Merritt laid out a plan to keep Three Rivers green and beautiful. It was the kind of positive message we rarely hear from civil servants these days. It made you feel proud of the city and confident that its trees—which most of us take for granted—were in good hands. Our public officials are usually too embattled by politics, or gun-shy of criticism, to speak with such candor about the work they do.

The conversation ended rather abruptly after Merritt got called about a minor crisis in downtown Three Rivers. Hard to say what it was about. All we heard was a burst of energetic squawking on his two-way radio.

One of his parting comments really stayed with me, though.

"Every lot in the city," he said, "Has a right to a tree. No matter who they are, they have a *right* to a tree."

This startled me because *right* is a strong word and meticulous Merritt is not one for hyperbole. For a government official to proclaim a right, especially one that not's codified in law, is risky business. So I called him on it.

"Wait a minute, you just said everyone has a 'right to a tree.' That's pretty radical for a place like Three Rivers. Do you really mean that?" I asked.

"Yes, *right* is a strong word, and, yes, I believe it," he said. "If you want a tree, you should *have* a tree. It's a quality of life issue. Trees and treed streets are that important."

Over the next few weeks, I took Merritt at his word. I drove the streets of Three Rivers but mainly in the poorer parts of town. I knew that a bank vice president in the prosperous First Ward could get city hall to plant trees in her yard. What about a single mom, living on WIC food coupons, in a dismal Second Ward rental property? How would she rate?

Well, I can report that she might rate a horse chestnut with spikes of showy red blooms in spring. Or a tulip tree with flowers as yellow-white as a magnolia. Or maybe a copper beech that will one day lend her humble yard the elegance of a European estate.

Sure, her roof might leak and the screen door might hang halfway off its hinges. The itinerant thugs who live next door might even turn their kitchen into a meth lab firetrap. But she would rate a tree because she deserved a tree, and if her little town could do this one hopeful thing to brighten her life then so be it. An engineer who loved trees would see to that.

FROM LOCAL ACORNS,
MIGHTY OAKS (AND
GORGEOUS GUITARS) GROW

For a few months one winter, when I was twenty years old, I was a
trapper. That's trapper, as in a person who, theoretically, catches fur-
bearing animals and sells their pelts for money. I was then unem-
ployed, and it seemed like a rustic and rugged way to make some
cash. It was certainly exhilarating. On icy mornings, with only my
grandpa's flimsy old hip waders for protection, I'd slip into the
Prairie River south of Three Rivers. With steely-eyed resolve, (it was
always my secret hope that someone would see me out there), I'd
check my traps for muskrat, mink, and raccoon.

To prepare myself, I'd read a library book on the subject and talked
with my friend Terry, who was an accomplished trapper. He sold
dozens of furs each year. I also visited my Uncle Harry, who let me
admire the red fox pelts he'd hung to dry from the rafters in his
garage. He was vague on specifics but assured me I'd get the hang of it.

Apparently, there was much that Terry/Harry had left unsaid.
After two long, cold months afield, I'd trapped a grand total of two
muskrats. Although I badly needed the ten dollars they'd bring, I
couldn't bear to sell them. The thought of ambling into the fur
buyer's office—with a single, measly pelt in each hand—was too
embarrassing to contemplate.

Many people today, especially urbanites, find trapping to be
repugnant. Yet in the late 1970s we'd never heard of PETA (or pita
for that matter). Trapping, like coon hunting, plowing snow, or cutting firewood, was an acceptable way for blue-collar folks with sea-

sonal jobs to supplement their skimpy unemployment checks. And that was my basic intent. Except that my secondary motive, which I dared not divulge at the time, was more esoteric. I wanted to model my life after that of Henry David Thoreau.

Earlier that year I'd found a battered copy of *Walden* in a box of junk my mother bought at a garage sale. Like millions of readers before me, the book's impact was immediate and profound. I readily identified with Thoreau's mystical love of nature. I relished his cranky independence and drop-dead rejection of materialism and social convention. For a time, I considered *Walden* a de facto instruction manual for my unfocused life. To live as truthfully and closely to the earth as one's circumstances would allow seemed liked the noblest of vocations. Especially when you're living at home, pumping gas and shoveling asphalt for the minimum wage.

But where it all broke down was in the harsh realm of practicality. As just one example, the big woods where I trapped had just gone on the market for $250,000. At the time, I earned about $6,000 annually and may have had $50 in savings. So just how and where could a modern person of humble means earn a living from nature's bounty? How could you even learn the skills necessary for such a life? My trapping enterprise was a failed but well-intended attempt to explore some of those questions.

More than twenty-five years later I'm still working on the answers. I suspect many who love nature but earn their living in the great indoors feel the same way. The things we're socially conditioned to want can tether us to jobs and situations that leave us comfortable but unfulfilled. I don't think it's quite true that most people live lives of "quiet desperation," as Thoreau said. In his fervent but celibate quest for purity, Henry often seemed a bit desperate himself. Still, if we had our druthers, many of us would find a vocational compromise that brings us closer to our ideals.

It's always heartening, then, when I find people near my home who have found a way to do just that. And I'm not talking here of hermit scholars cut from the cloth of Thoreau. Nor of brooding misfits who flee to the woods to harbor some dark grievance against humanity. Rather, these are back to nature entrepreneurs who, by living a sustainable lifestyle, profit themselves and the wider community.

Usually, they grow or make local things you can't buy anywhere else—honey, custom furniture, fresh strawberries, or hormone-free beef. Some do it full time, others as a sideline avocation. Their enterprise may not be lucrative, but somehow it succeeds—"right livelihood," the Buddhists call it. Once they put themselves in service of a higher ideal, things often fall into place almost organically.

Such a person is Jan Burda, who I met last fall at his country home in rural Berrien County, Michigan.

Perhaps the most overquoted and annoying philosophical question of our time is this: "If a tree falls in the woods and no one hears it, will it still make a sound?" Well, I can definitely say that in Jan Burda's woods it will—and with enough practice it might even sound like Elvis, Bill Monroe, or Bob Dylan. That's because Jan is one of the rare professionals who still make musical instruments by hand. Rarer still is that they're carved from native Michigan hardwoods that grow wild on his fifty-acre property.

"Why would I want to buy spruce wood from Germany," he asks, "when there's a downed sugar maple lying in the driveway?"

Jan is sixty-five and sports a gray ponytail. He's bespectacled and soft-spoken, with the slight, energetic stature of a shopkeeper. But his hands, with their calluses and a bruised purple thumbnail, betray his calling as a craftsman. He's built his own guitars and violins since 1968 and knows of no one else who makes them his way.

Then again, you won't find many people who are still made like Jan Burda, either.

He's a self-taught artisan and conservationist who also happens to be a firearms expert and bottler of home-brewed lager. He's a chemist and metallurgist who designed components for NASA's zero-gravity toilet. ("The astronauts should thank me every time they sit down.") He's a clever builder who has erected three sturdy, low-impact dwellings on his property. (One of these, a geodesic dome, is so durable that it may have to be razed with dynamite.)

For all his talents, perhaps Jan's greatest achievement is that he's found a way to root his life and career in the natural world around him. To see how he does it, I paid him a visit on a chilly November morning along with Pete DeBoer, a staff member with the Southwest Michigan Land Conservancy.

A small, hand-carved sign marks the Burda driveway, which narrows as it leads from the road through an overgrown field into the woods. It ends just shy of Jan's first architectural creation, a log cabin that he built with his father in 1970.

This isn't one of those high-varnish, Montana millionaire models with elk-antler chandeliers and sculpted granite countertops. With its low eaves and dark-hued logs, Jan's backwoods home hugs the earth like a Yukon trapper's cabin. Its compact size—four hundred square feet—leaves little room for wasted space or excess possessions.

"Been chopping wood," says Jan, by way of introduction. "Be with you after I throw another log on the fire."

For a better view of the landscape, we adjourn to his new building site. It overlooks a little valley that's heavily wooded with tall beeches—a southern mesic forest. Through the valley's heart winds Farmers Creek, a certified trout stream that supports annual runs of Coho salmon from Lake Michigan. In spring, the marshy ground blooms with a profusion of wildflowers that botanists say is unlike anything they've seen.

"It's incredible," says Pete DeBoer. "In most woods, you see a few clumps of trillium here and there. Out here they're so thick you can't walk without stepping on one."

In all, more than fifty species of wildflowers and trees have been found on the property. Jan says some parts of the valley were never logged due to the steep terrain. It's hard to believe that forty years ago most locals considered the parcel wasteland. In 1963, Jan's father bought the whole thing for less than one hundred dollars per acre.

"Back then if it wasn't tillable nobody wanted it," he says. "Now everybody would love to have it—so they could sell lots for million-dollar houses."

But such development will never happen because Jan has taken legal steps to prevent it. Through a conservation easement with the Southwest Michigan Land Conservancy, the land will remain a permanent nature preserve. The easement will stay in place even after the parcel changes hands. Jan gets a decent tax break from the deal but nothing like the huge chunk of cash he'd get if the land were sold for development.

In the meantime, he's free to use his land in a sustainable fashion.

He can hunt, fish, garden, harvest fallen trees for all manner of uses, and hold his locally famous bluegrass jam sessions (at which his home brew serves as a powerful social lubricant). It seems like the ideal situation, does it not? Live in a beautiful place, cut up a few trees now and Zen, and from that hew the stuff of a peaceful and purposeful life.

That's true now, but it's taken some extensive joinery to fit all the pieces together.

What's fascinating about Jan's journey to the woods is that he began his adulthood in left-brain pursuits. A Southwest Michigan native, he attended Hope College in Holland, Michigan (prelaw), and then worked as a chemist for Whirlpool, the giant appliance maker.

After a soul-searching road trip in the early 1970s, his career evolved into more right-brain occupations. For a time, he taught school in Berrien Springs, Michigan. Then, following his muse, he took a 180-degree turn and opened a music store in South Bend, Indiana. His success led him to open stores in Toronto and Chicago.

In Chicago, Burda spent (he would now say endured) his longest professional stint. For fifteen years, he owned and operated a music store on the north side. Over time, he found the confines and clamor of city life to be intolerable.

"I could lean out my window and touch my neighbor's house," he recalls. "If you grew up in a big city, you can accept that—just like you can accept hearing screams and sirens and gunshots all the time. But I had a problem with it."

Weekend trips to Michigan helped "feed his soul." He'd always kept ties to the family woodland and decided to build a geodesic dome there in the 1970s. They were all the rage then. As it was going up, farmers came from around the neighborhood to watch and shake their heads. They'd never seen a house built without corners.

There was one fatal flaw, though. At NASA, engineers designed domes for life on the moon, which gets considerably less rain then Southwest Michigan. With their many joints, the roofs invariably leak. This explains why the Burda dome, with its mossy, curled shingles and collapsed sidewalls, now squats crookedly on the forest floor like a giant toadstool. Given its design, the building is becoming more unified as it collapses on itself. At this point, it would be nearly impossible to disassemble it.

At any rate, in 1989 Jan decided he'd had enough of Chicago and moved back to Michigan for good. Since then, he's split his time between the cabin and his music store in downtown Berrien Springs.

Around home, his latest project is to complete the house he began on his property in 2006. It's an ecodwelling (no yard, just forest) that reflects his commitment to art and functionality. Its eight-inch-thick walls are made of poured concrete and will help maintain a steady indoor temperature. Inside, the main floor will consist of hand-cut wooden tiles fashioned from native black cherry. Outside, a coat of warm beige stucco will match the color of autumn beech leaves.

It's what you'd expect from a man who could well be described as a pragmatic tree hugger. "I love it when a tree falls," Jan says. "I'll either burn it for firewood or cut it up and make something useful of it."

Yet the place where his skill and artistry reaches its zenith is the music store. It's a far cry from the mainstream establishments he ran elsewhere. There are no compact discs, electric guitars, or amps for sale. There's barely room for a few racks of instruments and the band saws and belt sanders that he uses to make them. It's probably not much larger than the home-based pencil factory that Thoreau once ran so ably for his father.

On one wall of the music shop hangs a row of shiny acoustic models that Jan says are Martin guitar replicas. Elsewhere, unvarnished backs and necks cut from black cherry, walnut, and ironwood await their turn at perfection. All are fashioned from trees that drew their sustenance from the soil and sunshine of the local woods.

What these six-string beauties will someday sound like will be for musicians and their audiences to decide. But, no matter where they're played, it's certain that Jan Burda's creations will always echo the wild harmonies of his Southwest Michigan home.

THE NEW CIDERHOUSE RULES

To enjoy a chilled glass of fresh apple cider is one of the signature pleasures of a Michigan autumn. Since my wife's Uncle Dayton owns an orchard a few miles away, we keep a supply on hand from late September to at least Thanksgiving. To extend the season, we put several gallon jugs in the freezer. (Voice of experience: to prevent volcanolike eruptions of frozen cider, be sure to pour off a glass before freezing.)

In our estimation, what makes Dayton's cider so good is that it's fresh and unpasteurized. Fresh cider contains an organic cornucopia of vital nutrients and enzymes. Fresh cider has a winelike subtlety; each blend with its own distinct flavor and aroma. The best fresh cider has a golden sparkle, like fine amber from the Baltic Sea.

By comparison, pasteurized cider (the kind sold in most stores) has a flat and waxy taste. Its muddy texture and appearance resemble the rusty fluid that leaks from old radiators. And it doesn't get that way by accident. Pasteurized cider has been heat treated, to at least 160 degrees, to kill off any potentially dangerous microorganisms.

Yet traditionalists such as Dayton contend that pasteurization robs living cider of its natural vitality and health benefits. In the past forty years, Dayton has made and sold thousands of gallons of fresh cider. During that time, his homegrown product has never caused any reported health problems.

For the government, his good track record may no longer be good enough. The trouble began in 1996, when a one-year-old girl in

Washington died after drinking unpasteurized apple juice that was contaminated with E coli bacteria. Since then, regulations have grown tighter. The Food and Drug Administration (FDA) requires unpasteurized cider to carry a label that warns of its health risks to children, the elderly, and people with weak immune systems. In Michigan and elsewhere, farms that sell unpasteurized cider must now have regular inspections.

Each year, Dayton says, the inspectors who visit his orchard become more aggressive. They want him to follow more procedures, some of them costly, to guard against perceived health risks. For instance, farmers can no longer make cider from windfalls (washed apples that have fallen from the tree), a time-honored way to make full use of the harvest. The concern is that windfalls may have come in contact with animal feces that could contain E coli.

It's an old story in American agriculture. To remedy a new problem, the government creates a new set of regulations that tend to increase equipment and labor costs. For small farmers, ranchers, and food processors, these extra costs can be hard or impossible to bear. Yet wealthy corporate farms and multinational food corporations, whose lobbyists often help write the regulations, come out smelling like a rose. (Or, more accurately, a genetically modified rose that's been picked by exploited labor and flown halfway around the world on a fuel-guzzling cargo plane.)

When it comes to food safety, there's no question that government agencies have a crucial role to play. But there's something about their logic that doesn't add up. In Michigan, for example, there's never been a single reported death attributed to unpasteurized cider. Not one. And, no matter where you live, the chances of a healthy adult getting sick from fresh cider are infinitely small.

We do know, however, that heart disease is the nation's leading cause of death. It now kills some 650,000 people annually. We also know that a diet high in fresh fruits and vegetables helps deter heart disease and cancer. So for most people, the risks of *not* consuming enough foods such as fresh cider far exceed the risks of doing so. Still, I've yet to see warning labels about heart disease on the wrappers of half-pound monster burgers. Nor on the boxes of cardiac-clogging pizzas that feature four meat toppings, two cheeses, and even more

fatty cheese injected into the crust—a gluttonous practice that sounds a lot like reverse liposuction.

My larger theory (so far unproven) is that drinking fresh cider may even have an unintended halo effect. That's because the places that sell fresh cider are almost always like Dayton's orchard: small operations that offer a bounty of healthy, locally grown produce at affordable prices.

The open-air "porch" where Dayton sells his wares overlooks a jewel of a little lake that's bordered by woods and vineyards. My favorite time to visit is autumn when it takes on the classic air of a still life painting. The bins overflow with October beans, redskin potatoes, peaches, pears, plums, grapes, and half a dozen kinds of apples. Spanish onions hang in fragrant clumps from the rafters. The

shelves sag with luscious tomatoes, pendulous squashes, and volup-
tuous eggplants. It's a seductive sensory experience that's part shopping spree, part pagan harvest ritual. Along with cider, you can't help
but leave with a trunk load of the healthiest food God made this side
of the Euphrates River.

You will, of course, find well-stocked produce sections in the
chain grocery stores that sell pasteurized cider. But they sell far more
of the overprocessed, high-sugar, high-sodium crap that we Americans find so lethally alluring. Not so at a country produce stand. Usually, it's either the fresh stuff that's in season or nothing. As the sign
above Dayton's cash register proudly proclaims. "We Grow What We
Sell."

So all I'm saying to the government regulators is give us a choice
and a chance. Go ahead and affix the scarlet letter of a warning label
if you must. Just don't ban, overregulate, or unduly harass local folks
who sell good food that's rooted in their native environment and
economy. Lord knows we've got far too little of that as it is.

Three miles from Dayton's orchard there's a big supermarket
where we used to buy FDA-approved juice boxes for our children.
One day, after reading the label, I decided that was no longer a
good idea. What convinced me was this disclaimer: "This carton
may contain apple juice from the USA, Argentina, Chile, Germany,
or Austria."

May contain? Not does contain, or will contain, but *may* contain.
Had the lawyers who wrote this been injected with truth serum perhaps they'd have said something like this: "We, the rootless corporation that produced this product, have only the vaguest idea where
your food came from. But if bad apples poison the juice we're reasonably confident that we can narrow down our source to three of
the world's seven continents. "

Call me middle-aged crotchety, but I'll take my chances with Dayton's fresh cider any day. I know it comes from fruit that he's planted,
tended, and feeds to his own family. For me, that's assurance enough.
Because a life that strives for zero risk is a lot like pasteurized cider:
it has little color, even less flavor, and a bad aftertaste that makes you
long for the real thing.

"TREES" FOR SALE

Every so often that amorphous blob we call "the government" cre-ates something so well conceived, so important, and so beneficial to its citizens that you wonder how they pulled it off. The national park system, the Peace Corps, and even the U.S. Marine Corps come to mind.

But on the local level, when it comes to good government, it's hard to top the annual conservation district tree sale. Every tree it sells is affordably priced. You can buy as few as one or as many as a thousand. In the true Jeffersonian spirit, this means that any person with a few extra dollars and a shovel can help create a citizen-planted leafocracy. It's a social program even conservatives can love since cit-izens assume all the work and obligation. Although the trees will grow on private property, the public will share in the clean air, clean water, and improved wildlife habitat they help provide.

Annual tree sales, and conservation districts, were established by President Franklin Roosevelt after the dust bowl of the 1930s. They were formed as a front line of defense against the erosion and destructive farming practices that had laid waste to much of the nation's cropland. In this desperate time, both farmers and the Amer-ican public had to relearn an ancient lesson, that without healthy top-soil human survival becomes a tenuous proposition.

Today there are some three thousand conservation districts nationwide. They go by various names, but all offer services that help farmers, ranchers, and landowners to practice soil and water conser-vation in ways large and small.

Yet for every well-intended government policy there's always a lowest common denominator, the point where rhetoric meets reality. Whatever the mission or program may be, progress won't happen without grunts on the ground to do the dirty work.

On this bright April morning in Centreville, Michigan, those grunts are us. They consist of three volunteers: me and two other guys I didn't know until a few minutes ago. Meanwhile, up front taking tree orders are two paid (albeit underpaid) staff members of the St. Joseph County Conservation District.

It's cold enough to see your breath, and we're standing on a cement floor in a long, wooden barn at the St. Joseph County Fairgrounds. All around us are waist-high sacks of tree seedlings. There's white oak, red oak, black cherry, white spruce, red and white pine, serviceberry, dogwood, sugar maple, sycamore, and a baffling little shrub known as ninebark.

It's a simple operation. We get an order, pick out the seedlings, pack their roots in wet sphagnum moss—it's even colder than it sounds—and wrap them in a bundle of sturdy brown paper. Since it's almost Earth Day, who could ask for a better bouquet?

In five years as a volunteer, this is the most successful tree sale I've seen. For one thing, we've devised a strategic new customer enticement strategy: free coffee and doughnuts. We've also started to sell trees individually. In the past, ten was the minimum order since most buyers were farmers or people with large chunks of land who wanted a windbreak or tree plantation. That's no longer the case. The average customer now owns a house on a few acres in the country. For them, ten trees is about five too many.

Our enhanced marketing efforts may have been too successful. An hour earlier, while I was working alone, we fell way behind on orders. We'd never been this busy before. A line of twenty fidgety customers curled out the front door and onto the sidewalk.

Then something happened that you'll never see during a rush hour at Wal-Mart. Within fifteen minutes of each other, two volunteers appeared out of nowhere to offer assistance. The first was Marco, a teenaged exchange student from Bulgaria dressed in a soccer jersey. Seriously. Of all the places in the world Marco could have been, this was surely among the least likely. The other guy, Larry, got restless waiting in line and came back to help. Larry, who said he'd recently won a battle with cancer, seemed eager for the chance to do something that bespoke of new life.

Once we had ample manpower on hand, another crisis surfaced. We ran out of brown paper in which to wrap the trees. As closing time approached, we scrounged every possible material we could find—newspapers, burlap, ragged sheets of black plastic, and even those flimsy white plastic grocery bags. Everything. We shut the barn door at 1:00 p.m. on the nose, with no wrapping materials left. Our mystery volunteers, their karmic debts repaid, were free to leave.

The barn fell suddenly quiet. I felt cold, tired, and hungry but satisfied. (Note to self: hide box of white-powdered doughnuts for me next year.) As always, I wondered what would happen to all those bundles people took home that day. Especially the guy who splurged for 250 Carolina poplars, certain that a willing brother-in-law or nephew would help put them in. How many of those would make it into the ground?

That enthusiasm, even if short-lived, is part of what makes the tree sale so heartening. Because, when you think about it, we don't really sell trees. A scraggly, leafless, brown object whose diameter barely exceeds that of a pencil cannot in good conscience be called a tree. Not yet. No, what we actually sell is hope—the promise of forests and shade trees yet to come. Along with mulch and water, it takes a good measure of human imagination to help them survive.

At a tree sale a few years ago, I was at the counter when a perky, middle-aged woman came in. She'd ordered from our catalog, so her prepacked bundle was one of many that waited in long rows on the floor. Evidently, this was her first tree sale.

"So, should I pull up to the door out back?" she chirped. "I borrowed a pickup with a trailer, and I brought a friend along to help load them up!"

She was here to get twenty-five redbud trees. Redbuds are notable for their purple-pink blossoms and rarely exceed twenty feet in height. They're native to the eastern deciduous forest but do well as a yard tree, preferably in light shade. Twenty-five such trees, as envisioned in the mind's eye, would certainly occupy a lot of space.

But the twenty-five redbud seedlings I brought her? They could have fit neatly into a child's hand.

"That's it?" she cried. "Those are my trees? Oh, my!"

She let her friend carry the "trees" as they walked sheepishly back to her empty three-quarter-ton pickup truck. The one with an empty flatbed trailer attached.

They were, nonetheless, her redbud trees, encoded with all the genetic instructions needed to someday become the ornamental beauties of her dreams. And for the time being they had the added virtue of extreme portability. With a little shove, she could probably even fit them under the front seat.

Forgotten Waters

A BLESSING BESIDE
AND BENEATH ME

It was an August evening along the wooded shores of Lake Four in St. Joseph County, and a chorus of bullfrogs was thar-rumping across the lily pads. We were fishing the tea-colored waters for bass, flipping plastic worms and Hula Poppers into the shallows. When we heard the clank of oars, we looked up to see a baldheaded, Benedictine monk rowing toward us in a johnboat. In adolescent male fashion, we tried to appear cool and nonchalant.

"Good evening, boys."

"Evenin'."

"Do you know this is a private lake? How did you get on here?"

"We came in through the channel," I said. "My Uncle George lives on the swampy half of the lake, and that's where we put in."

"Well, I must ask you to leave."

"Well, my dad says you can't kick somebody off a lake if they got water access. That's the state law. He says nobody can make you leave."

Silence.

The monk, who suddenly looked tired, rowed back across the lake toward St. Gregory's Abbey without saying another word. He never bothered Daryl and me again—perhaps he lacked the desire to argue common law with a couple of wiseacre fourteen year olds. There are reasons why middle-aged men don robes and commit themselves to monasteries.

That was thirty years ago, and I'm still not sure if the law was on my

side. But I am confident that public opinion was. Like most Michigan citizens, I consider free access to lakes and rivers as a birthright. It's hard for us to fathom the western states' legal system, which allows water and water rights to be sold separately from the land like pork bellies on the Chicago Mercantile Exchange. You might as well mount light meters on trees and charge people for the sunshine.

In Michigan, there's no reason to be stingy about water: The state has 11,037 lakes and thirty-six thousand miles of rivers and streams. Just as Alaska's Inuit people have fifteen words for snow, so do Michiganders employ a rich vocabulary to describe their abundance. The terms *bog, marsh, fen, brook, stream, creek, river, pond, flooding, impoundment, lake,* and *big lake* each denote a distinct landscape and ecosystem.

It was by water routes that Europeans first explored the Great Lakes. In the 1670s, the French explorer LaSalle traveled through southern Michigan via the St. Joseph River. On sleepless nights, I've planned in my head a canoe trip to retrace the Old Northwest traders' route. A mile from my home is the Portage River, and from there I could follow a downstream passage all the way to the Gulf of Mexico.

The portage empties into the St. Joseph in Three Rivers, and at the St. Joe's "south bend" in northern Indiana I'd make the five-mile portage (though not on foot as LaSalle's party did) to the Kankakee River. Then I'd paddle the Kankakee until it joins the Illinois River and float the Illinois until it meets the Mississippi.

Rivers have always inspired freedom of thought and movement. Yet it's on lakes that Michiganders indulge the high passions of summer. Can a Michigan childhood truly be complete without a lakeside vacation? Our beloved cottages, with their lumpy beds and musty furniture, are clapboard shrines for generations of memories. The Zebco and bluegill mornings with grandpa, the grilled bratwurst and strawberry shortcake picnics, the secret thrills of bikini tan lines and late-night swims to a carpeted raft. It's no wonder that lake-vacation snapshots claim so much page space in Michigan photo albums.

There are other waters, too, but they are invisible reservoirs, eternally cold and dark. They are essential to life, although you'll never hear them mentioned in tourism ads. These are Michigan's underground seas, the aquifers that provide drinking water for about half of the state's residents. And what a remarkable, unsung resource they are. Despite all the forests and wetlands we've destroyed, and all the air and surface water we've polluted, the good earth abides. At the turn of a spigot, many of us can still draw water that's safe and untreated from the ground beneath our feet.

My wife's Uncle Roy lives in Blacksburg, Virginia, where he builds houses in the Blue Ridge Mountains. As he describes it, to dig a well in Appalachia is a hard and uncertain geological undertaking—up to 150 feet of expensive casing blasted through rock and clay to reach who knows what. Roy was astounded to hear that my brother Jeff, who lives down the road from me, had sunk his own well and struck water at 12 feet. It took Jeff about an hour, and he did the "drilling" himself by pounding a sleeve of weighted steel pipe. His own water supply, more than he will ever need, right beneath his feet and free for the taking. In much of the world, what a miracle that would be.

When I was eight years old and living in Florida, my northern cousins came to visit for the holidays. I recall reading with pride the slogan on their beige Michigan license plate: "Water-Winter Wonderland." We were moving back to Michigan soon, and the excitement captured by those three words said it all. And they have never disappointed. I am still enchanted with all that flows around, beside, and beneath me.

ANOTHER BEND IN THE RIVER

About a mile from my home, in the humble village of Parkville, there's a bridge across the Portage River. It's an appealing enough place but certainly not remarkable. From the bridge, you can see the footings of a fieldstone millrace, relics of the water-powered machinery that once ran a nineteenth-century flour mill. The river below widens into a pool that's ringed with reeds and half-sunken logs. It's the type of public waterfront where the angling proletariat likes to congregate. The power lines overhead are festooned with a fool's bounty of hooks, bobbers, and monofilament bird's nests.

A gravel footpath leads to a canoe landing where the current runs clear and cool. Still, there's enough ambient clutter to give the place a roughneck, if not redneck, air. It's not uncommon to find a few loaded diapers fermenting in the tall grass and a hastily discarded pair of black NASCAR panties.

But for me this minor surfeit of rubbish can do nothing to alter a basic truth: that in all the world there's no inanimate thing I love more than this gentle, unassuming river. And there's nowhere on earth where I'd rather spend an hour, day, week, or even eternity.

It's not that I've suffered for want of comparisons. Like many of my frequent-flyer generation, I've visited dozens of states and countries for business and pleasure. But on restless nights, when I couldn't sleep in Johannesburg, Shanghai, or São Paulo, I found that my mind and spirit always fled to here. To this gravel-bottomed stream, to this little woods on the riverbank where, on summer nights, ivory shafts of moonlight make the oak trunks glow like pillars in a temple.

You might dismiss these mental forays as a psychological coping device or as stress-reduction therapy for a lonely guy with jet lag who's trying to find his happy place. They've certainly worked well for that.

But these reasons alone can't explain my deep attraction to the river, nor can they begin to fathom its mysterious workings in my life. For at three distinct periods of growth and crisis the course of the river and I have intersected. Only recently, after the third encounter, has the pattern of this relationship become apparent. Of this much I am now certain: whenever I've returned to the river, it has redirected my life in ways that now seem providential. It also helped rescue me from a failed career as a small-town furnace mechanic. But more on that shortly.

A NEAR PLACE WHERE NO ONE GOES

The first encounter is still the most memorable. I am twelve years old, a skinny, timid kid who loves books but gets terrible grades, who loves baseball but has little athletic ability. It's the summer of 1972, Rod Stewart's "Maggie May" is my favorite song, and my friends and I are whiling away the afternoon on a scruffy schoolyard diamond.

Then, from the outfield, I see a sight that jolts me out of my adolescent torpor. It's Brent Morris, a neighborhood kid who lives with his mom and brother in a drab house by the railroad tracks. He's lanky and broad across the shoulders and can whack a baseball far and high. Yet he keeps to himself and rarely joins in our sandlot games. And perhaps here's why: larger than life, he comes sloshing down the street in wet shorts and muddy sneakers, a Huck Finn demigod with a full stringer of smallmouth bass and northern pike slung over his shoulder.

Brent's separateness was never so evident, and admirable, as on that clear June day. We'd been playing baseball—typical midwestern kid stuff. We could scarcely imagine doing anything but that. Meanwhile, Brent had gone off alone and done an adult thing that none of us would do or could do. He'd waded down a dark river and somehow caught a remarkable mess of fish. The men we knew would respect him greatly for that.

I reached out and touched the fish in a curious, tentative way. I smelled my hand, now sticky with slime, and recoiled at first from the fishiness. Walking home, my hand returned to my nose again and again—the musky scent enticed me.

I'd fished before, yet Brent's experience was far removed from the sedate trips I'd taken with my dad to catch bluegills on Fisher Lake. This wading business had a hint of social rebellion about it. Although I lived in a town named Three Rivers, most white people thought our three rivers were dirty and unsafe. Only hillbillies and "colored folks" on River Road ate fish from the rivers. I'd never seen anyone, black or white, set foot in these waters. Except for Brent. And now, more than anything, I wanted to join him.

A week later Brent agreed to take me wading down the Portage River. As a starting point, he chose the tail waters beneath the Boys Dam. It's a small dam, perhaps eight feet tall and one hundred feet wide, but with the water still high from spring rains the boiling, thigh-deep current was plenty treacherous. Initially, the whole idea seemed crazy. How could anyone even walk here without drowning? I took my cues from Brent, who was fearless in his maroon cutoff shorts and Kmart sneakers. Within seconds, he'd hooked a writhing bass, which he proudly hoisted for my benefit from the foam-flecked river.

Fifty yards below the Boys Dam, the river turns sharply to the south. It's quiet enough to hear downy woodpeckers at work in the basswood trees, and it was here that Brent taught me my first lesson in river fishing. "In a river," he said, "the fish face upstream, 'cause that's where their food comes from."

Brent demonstrated with a gold Mepps spinner how to cast upstream in the proper two o'clock or ten o'clock direction. The Mepps is a beautiful piece of functional hardware, with a brass blade about the size of a baby spoon that pivots above a treble hook that's often dressed in deer or squirrel hair. When fished correctly, a Mepps comes wobbling downstream like a sluggish minnow—irresistible prey for a game fish. The tricky part is to retrieve it at the same speed as the current. Reel too fast and the spinner's blade will barely turn. Reel too slow and the three-pointed hook will be forever getting snagged on the logs, rocks, and clams that lie on the bottom.

Until then, I'd fished on lakes surrounded by acres of open water. I'd tie on my dad's heaviest lure and cast two-handed like a surf fisherman, just to see how big a splash I could make. Kid stuff. But here, within the first thirty minutes, I lost four lures. They hung like Christmas tree ornaments from the branches overhead, forever unrecoverable. The moral was clear: this was no place to screw around. I was a barber's son, and the fifteen dollars in tackle I lost that morning would not soon be replaced. In my dad's words, I was SOL—shit out of luck.

Nevertheless, Brent had faith in his hapless pupil. "Don't worry," he said, loaning me some tackle from his own meager supply. "You'll catch your limit before we're through." He was wrong about that. I didn't catch a single legal-sized fish that day, and it would be years before I attained the expertise he took for granted. But about everything else—the sensory pleasures of wading, the thrill of standing in a river while a fish splashes and dashes in the water around you—he was absolutely right.

At the time, I couldn't appreciate the depth of what Brent had done for me. For the next few years, the river would be about the only place where I would excel and achieve. To master the art of pinpoint casting, to step boldly in roiling waters, to clean fish on the back porch under my father's approving eye, all this brought confidence and joy to the uncertain world of adolescence.

Because of Brent, I came to know a wild and forgotten local landscape that was virtually mine to explore. The two rivers I waded, the Portage and the nearby Rocky, were both a five-minute walk from home. Even as a twelve year old, I could see that these waters were neither dirty nor unsafe. They were worthy of reverence and affection. They teemed with fish, mammals, reptiles, amphibians, and croaky blue herons. In the muggy twilight, when silver wreaths of mist rose from the Rocky River marsh, the world looked as fresh as the first evening of the first day.

My apprenticeship was brief, however. We only waded together two or three times before Brent slipped off on his own again. I was kind of miffed at first, but I came to see that he was right. On a small Michigan river, he fishes best who fishes alone.

The second encounter, like so much from the late 1970s, still seems a bit hazy. I am twenty years old and have just returned to the river, but I am not exactly sure why.

I feel as if I've just awakened in a strange place after a party. Or, in my case, after a three-year party. Many of my high school friends had left Three Rivers for college, never to return. The blue-collar guys who I've since befriended all have decent-paying jobs as skilled tradesmen. They're buying cool cars and houses and are taking long bubble baths with their girlfriends. Meanwhile, I'm living at home with a minimum wage job. My 1.9 high school grade point average has left me with few other options.

For six months, I had a respectable factory job at a United Auto Workers plant in Three Rivers that made springs for the auto industry. But I was fired due to sarcasm, sloth, and tardiness. (And it took some doing, in the late 1970s, for a union worker in Michigan to be fired for anything short of multiple homicide.)

For a young man with little personal initiative, the solution to this vocational dilemma seemed clear. I, too, would become a tradesman. As my father advised, "It was time that I learned to do something with my hands."

Little did I know that this, my first calculated career move, would turn me into a contemplative fisherman.

My mentor was a seventy-eight-year-old furnace repairman named Porky who my dad knew from his barbershop and the Elks Club. Despite his Depression era nickname, Porky was bald, rail thin, and chain smoked Phillip Morris cigarettes. I was supposed to be Porky's apprentice except that he was too impatient to be much of a teacher. And I, given to narcoleptic episodes of daydreaming, was a lousy student.

In lieu of mentorship, I was Porky's gofer. Instead of learning a trade, as my friends were doing, I was relegated to grunt work. I threaded steel gas pipe with a hand die, demolished radiators with a sledgehammer, and bludgeoned fifty-year-old octopus furnaces into flattened piles of sheet metal and asbestos dust. With violent imprecision, I would wield mauls, chisels, and crowbars to shatter cast iron pipe fittings or hack new register holes in the hardwood floors of old houses.

As it turned out, the job with Porky was right, though for all the wrong reasons. Porky had a wise, if somewhat taciturn, way about him. I'd just come from a factory where the young guys snuck out to smoke dope during lunch breaks. The conversations tended to revolve around four-barrel carburetors and female anatomy. By comparison, Porky's willingness to discuss politics and current affairs seemed almost scholarly. Since Porky paid poverty wages, I hadn't the means to repair my broken-down hot-rod. (I'd blown its engine while roaring down a country road at 110 miles per hour.)

With little beer money and no girlfriend, my opportunities for recreation were limited. So, as May turned to June, an agreeable thought came to mind: why not go down again to the river?

For much of that summer, my workdays ended with a pleasant ritual at the side yard spigot. With the cicadas buzzing in the treetops, I'd scrub my face and arms until the cobwebs, sawdust, and pipe shavings vanished in a gray lather onto the sidewalk. By the forsythia bushes were the old sneakers I'd set out to dry the night before. I am 6 feet 5 inches tall, and after a day of stooping about in farmhouse basements I was eager to feel the limitless sky above my head. After supper—and, as virtuous midwesterners, we never ate later than 6:00 p.m.—I'd slip on my wading shoes, still warm from the afternoon sun, and head for one of the rivers of home.

By this time, I'd learned to wade with a minimum of cargo: a small bottle of insect repellent and a plastic bag with three or four spinners. I rarely kept fish to eat except for big pike, and on those occasions I'd use one of my shoelaces for a stringer. When I had to cut fishing line, I'd use my two front teeth. (At age thirty, when I finally got a job with health insurance, a dentist x-rayed my teeth and asked what had caused all those tiny stress fractures.)

I began to fish the wildest stretches of the Portage River, which were a few miles out of town. Most magical was a quarter-mile section where downed trees made the river impassable to boats and canoes. It was a solitary garden of shaded pools where big fish hid in the amber waters.

On summer evenings, the river was a movable feast for the senses.

Beneath high scalloped clouds and an aquamarine sky, I'd see not only herons but ducks, geese, hawks, kingfishers, and a rainbow of songbirds—warblers, tanagers, indigo buntings, and orioles. Sometimes I'd startle a herd of deer, which would tear through the marsh with a primal crash that echoed through the trees like artillery.

To reach the best holes, I'd crawl over the slimy, half-submerged trunks of downed willows and silver maples, my shins scraped and bruised by hidden roots and branches, my shoes painfully impacted with river gravel, my face and arms welted by mosquito and deerfly bites. Somehow it all seemed satisfying. It was a time for learning hard things, for honing mind and body for the reckoning of adulthood.

The fishing itself was remarkable. In the best holes, a fat smallmouth bass would snatch my spinner on nearly every cast. Then, in a head-shaking leap it would rise, red gills and olive flanks aflash in a halo of mist and light. On a good evening I'd catch and release fifty fish. Although I was rarely more than a few hundred yards away from the nearest house, this hidden paradise was always mine alone.

How could a person see and do such things, night after night, and not be changed? Gradually, the river helped to heighten my senses and deepen my perceptions. Its soothing nature also made me more attuned to other enriching pastimes.

Almost on a bet, I'd gone running one night with my brother. It

nearly killed me—too many Twinkies in the factory lunchroom—but we kept at it and were soon logging twenty miles a week. After a midsummer evening on the river, it was exhilarating to run the tree-lined streets of Three Rivers, striding shirtless through cool shadows to the next island of a streetlight's glow.

The reflective hours spent on the river also fueled a resurgent interest in reading. I rediscovered the public library and began to consume books as if to overcome a long-ignored vitamin deficiency. Over the course of that summer, the fishing, running, and reading began to feed on one another. They provided a new stamina and clarity of mind, something to ponder during the doldrum days with Porky. My reading program progressed to include the usual freshman English fare: Henry David Thoreau, Sherwood Anderson, William Faulkner, and James Fenimore Cooper. On the river, I'd spend hours casting on autopilot as my mind mulled over a Sinclair Lewis novel or Nick Adams story by Ernest Hemingway. I *was* Nick Adams.

Such classics might have seemed irrelevant to bored college kids. But right in front of me I saw that Lewis's *Babbitt* and *Main Street* were dead-on satires of the small town that I called home. Sometimes at lunch Porky would take me to the Elks Club bar for a drink. We'd elbow in alongside civic boosters and small-bore braggarts who could've come straight from Gopher Prairie, Minnesota, circa 1910. There I'd sit, a minimum-wage serf in filthy blue jeans, feeling smug as I mentally compared George Babbitt to the town's middle-class elite. A little knowledge truly is a dangerous thing.

It would be tidy if this particular lesson from the river ended here: Confused young man returns to his boyhood refuge of the river, a journey that inspires him to begin a self-styled program of fitness and intellectual rehab. That's plausible enough, even if the results were less than earth shaking. It's easy to see how the solitude and serenity of wading could lead to a deeper sense of physical and mental awareness.

What's harder to grasp is how time spent on the river can shape the soul. Which is why, even after twenty-five years, there's a postscript to this story that I've yet to understand. I suppose that most people would classify it as a spiritual experience. That may be the case, except that it seemed so real, and so self-evident, that it hardly compares to the usual gold shaft of light epiphanies.

All I can say is this. For one week in spring, about the time that northern pike come upriver to spawn, there was a curious incident that I can only describe as the Presence.

While I don't recall exactly when it began, I remember quite clearly what if felt like. Imagine that you're working at a desk, reading or writing, and someone comes up and just stands there. They don't say anything. You don't say anything. Neither of you even looks at the other. There is no visual recognition or sound of any kind. There is, nonetheless, no doubt at all that someone is there.

That's how it felt, except that the visitor was inside my head. The Presence wasn't hostile, or even spooky, it was . . . simply . . . undeniably . . . there. It felt just as real as a handclasp to the shoulder.

It was at first unnerving. After a few days, it became like a lingering dinner guest who doesn't understand that you're tired and want go to bed.

Because it wouldn't leave, I decided to talk to it.

"So what do you want?" I asked tentatively. "Do you want me to go be a priest or something?"

I could think of no other reason why God—if that's who it was— would make himself known to a perpetually misguided young Catholic male. Since the priesthood scared me as much as anything, I decided to make a case for my current vocation.

"But I really *like* working on furnaces," I said aloud. "It's what I want to do. And what's wrong with doing that?"

The Presence didn't answer. But in the tradition of Lady Macbeth (I'd browsed a secondhand set of Shakespeare) I had indeed protested too much. In listening to my own voice, I detected a troubling insincerity about my present career choice. And, while it wasn't the cosmic boot in the ass that I really needed, it did get me thinking.

A day or so later, after perhaps achieving the end for which it was sent, the Presence faded away. It has never returned with such force, but often I wish that it would.

THE LONG WALK HOME

The third encounter with the river, at least by my reckoning, shouldn't have been necessary at all.

I am forty-five years old, and the river has done its work. It has led me from the stagnant backwater of postadolescence into the mainstream of a wider, more fulfilling, adult life. Eventually, the campaign of river-inspired reading gave me enough confidence to enroll in a community college and then to earn a bachelor's degree. This, in turn, has led to a job (with spotless restrooms no less) in the public affairs department of a multi-billion-dollar organization in which people are actually paid to talk and write.

Thus anchored to middle-class stability, my wife and I moved back to Three Rivers on our own terms. Our farmhouse stands about a mile from the river, and we even purchased a small campsite on the river's bank.

But, truth be told, we never camp there anymore. We've gotten too busy with work, young children, and house projects. Don't fish much, either. Privately, I tell myself (with some self-congratulation) that I've outgrown such ordinary pursuits. My outdoor interests have grown more erudite and diffuse. I fancy myself a budding naturalist, more interested in studying trees, plants, and wildflowers than slinging fish on a stringer.

What matters most now is to mine the rich vein of experience the river has given me. At nights and on weekends, there are outdoor stories to write for magazines and newspapers; commentaries about nature to deliver on public radio. There are board meetings and writing conferences to attend, where learned people drink bottled water and hold forth on an abstract thing they call "the environment."

It seems grand, this life of the mind, this heady pursuit of knowledge and public acclaim. Except that there isn't much peace or rest in it. Nor is there much visceral connection to the natural world—to the struggles of human muscle against finned flesh, to the earthly delights of golden-brown pike filets that you've caught and carved with your own hand. My passion for nature had gone flabby around the midsection.

And once you've known wildness do you know what it's like to live without it? Do you know what that does to a person? To deny yourself—for the cheap coin of career ambition—those sacred hours on the water? To forgo the simple joy of being saturated by the river, awash in life's most basic element, as the weeds caress your legs and the atoms of crayfish and glaciers filter into your pores and pockets? To forget how, as a half-submerged *Homo sapiens,* you've slipped at arm's length past muskrats, snakes, and wading deer that see you as just another natural facet of creation?

Your conscious mind may forget this for a while, but once hooked you can never really let it go. And know this: the river and your inner self—your true self—will conspire to bring you home.

I was trying to complete a monster corporate communications project, and after two years the stress had pushed me to the breaking point. Each time the end seemed near, more assignments were piled on and the deadline was extended by another month. Even away from work, I was unable to find relief in the usual sanctuary of my quiet country home. I had prostituted my love of nature into a part-time, free-lance writing job that brought ample pressures of its own.

As I would soon learn, if you refuse to rest long enough, your body will eventually take matters into its own hands. One winter night, while on a long walk to burn off nervous energy, everything simply revved out of control—and stayed there. It was a full-blown panic attack. It felt like the time my accelerator pedal stuck to the floor while I was driving ninety miles per hour in my 1970 Roadrunner. This time around, however, there was no emergency brake.

"Man, you are burned out—crispy fried," said my doctor the next day. "How long you been like this? You think you're Superman, with a big red *S* on your chest, or something?"

He ordered me to take the next two months off work for extreme exhaustion—March and April. Perversely enough, when you're given time to rest for exhaustion, rest is the one thing you *can't* do. There's too much anxiety, night terrors, and migraine headaches for that. About all you can do is watch the bird feeder and listen to your teeth chatter from nervous tension.

As the final insult, despite all my free time, I couldn't enjoy the stacks of good books that I'd always planned to read once my other work was done. My brain was worn out. To read anything more complex than a phone book caused great mental anguish.

The one exception, I was surprised to learn, was fishing magazines. What a cruel joke that was. I'd long since quit reading such mainstream publications whose hook and bullet writing I derided as dull and clumsy.

That was about to change. To read honest, practical stories with such titles as "Jigging for Spring Walleyes" was now a balm for my frazzled mind, sweet revenge against the literary pretense that had corroded my soul.

And as might be expected, when it was warm enough to wade, I returned again to the river.

After an absence of several years, the first few trips were a bit shaky. I tired easily and stumbled over mossy rocks and submerged logs. My casting was off. Like a reincarnation of my twelve-year-old self, I haplessly snagged lures in low-hanging branches.

Then, slowly, as the river worked its medicine, the old rhythms returned. Walk and cast, walk and cast; the crunch-crunch of footsteps on the gravel streambed; the brassy flash of the spinner tumbling through the tea-colored water.

As the weeks of summer passed, something unexpected happened. I began to see new patterns emerge in the water and to intuit things about fish habitat and behavior that a younger me had not understood. Chalk it up, if you will, to the calming powers of Xanax or the long-term benefits of the Clean Water Act. Whatever the reason, in two months I caught more fish, and more big fish, than I had in the last ten years. I felt a little better, too. Give it time, and the river's tranquility can't help but soak into your skin.

By the time Labor Day arrives in southern Michigan, the staghorn sumacs start to turn flame red in the fencerows. In the crown of our centenarian sugar maple, a caucus of starlings makes noisy travel plans for the coming trip south. And there's no longer enough daylight, after the supper dishes are cleared, for a long night on the water. The best I could hope for was a brief outing to close the season.

After work on a Tuesday, I hustled down to the Parkville Bridge for a short wade upstream. Dusk had fallen quickly, pink hued and somber, as it does in early September. Gone was the lingering azure twilight of June and July. Yet, while the air was cool, the water was still warm enough to yield the last fruits of summer.

It was almost dark when, from some hidden estuary of the galaxy, a massive hatch of mayflies swept in. They clung to my hair, arms and dampened T-shirt. They rose and fell in a cloud of frantic abandonment, frenzied by their desire to copulate and die before death claimed them. The fish, of course, went berserk. They slurped down the fragile insects like pigs at the trough, smacking their tails and rolling excitedly in the swift current below the dam.

The next fifteen minutes were what a fisherman dreams of when he tries to imagine heaven. In an ecstasy of nonstop action, I caught and released fish after fish—little bass, medium-sized bass, and big bass of a size I'd never encountered there before.

The largest of these, a full-bodied, eighteen-inch smallmouth, I caught last. It began with a gentle tug that escalated seconds later into the night's grand finale, a pitched battle between two predators.

For a few enraptured moments, we faced off like competing vectors in a physics problem. It was my skill, and six-foot spinning rod, pitted against the noblest, meanest creature the river could offer. As the reigning brute of his watery kingdom, he seemed enraged to find himself on the wrong side of the equation. He made three slashing runs. He bulldogged for the bottom. He tail-danced across the water, showering me with his ablutions.

I fought him in concentric circles, tightening the arc as he tired, doing just as Brent had taught me.

Finally, in a now practiced move, I grabbed his fleshy lower lip and hoisted him skyward, a three-pound offering of bronze-gold brilliance framed in silhouette against the setting sun. After taking his measure—literally and figuratively—I set him free to fight and breed again. But in my mind's eye I'll forever see us both frozen there: him shimmering with wild energy, me reduced to tears by the healing power of nature's grace.

"As a rule," Herman Hesse once said, "the bad, stupid periods of my life have agreed with me more than the reasonable and seemingly successful ones." I don't know if Hesse—a frail, chain-smoking German intellectual—ever had to step into the same river thrice like I did. Nonetheless, I think he'd agree that an occasional meander from the status quo, if not always healthy, is in many ways necessary.

As for me, the fisherman, the tree hugger, and the preening writer inside have struck a compromise. They concur that, while it's fine to fish with single-minded obsession, it's also important to have the vision and perspective of a naturalist. It deepens your enjoyment of the river to know the swamp white oaks and sycamores, the wood-land sunflowers and blue lobelia. Miss that and you might as well be casting into a plastic trout pond at the mall.

It's also a privilege to share one's outdoor experiences through writing. But not everything you think or do should be turned into words and thus into money. Writing should be subordinate to experience, the distilled essence of a life well lived. Everyone must have places in the world, and places inside themselves, that are inviolate.

One summer twenty-five years ago I bragged to a friend that no one in the world knew the river like I did. Then the next spring there came a flood that filled the familiar holes with sand and swept away the old logjams and hiding places. It was all quite unsettling. My eyes and feet had to relearn a whole new geography. I had to apply the lessons I'd learned from the old river to the new one.

I'm sure the route ahead will include another unseen bend or two. Maybe even a few deep holes or sandbars. But who would have it any other way? A life, like a river, must forever adjust its course or else risk the sedimentation of dreams and desire.

Winter, Death, and Other Country Pleasures

DEATH OF A SMALL TOWN SALESMAN

You couldn't see how long the procession was until it turned east onto Moorepark Road. From a half mile back, across a field hazy green with shoots of rye, it looked like a Fourth of July parade. There were sheriff and police cars with flashing red and blue lights. In the lead was a round-nosed fire truck, the kind still used by rural volunteers. From a distance, you couldn't read the little orange and black flags that fluttered on the front fenders. The only clue was the Cadillac hearse that carried the casket of my friend's father, the man everyone called Tom Sr.

When I saw the stream of cars, I couldn't help but think of Willy Loman from the play *Death of a Salesman*. For Loman, neurotic daydreams were the only escape from a failed life of family scandal and wasted opportunity. In one especially pathetic scene, he envisions a glorious salesman's funeral that was almost identical to Tom Sr.'s: a standing room only crowd at the funeral home and a long motorcade that wound with slow dignity to the cemetery.

Tom Sr. was a salesman, but it's doubtful that he harbored any Lomanesque fantasies. He was too grounded in reality for that. He'd seen horrific combat at age seventeen and had spent most of his working life selling feed products to hog farmers—farming and soldiering being two occupations that keep one honest about one's place in the world.

Nonetheless, this common man did receive uncommon recognition. The dozens of friends and neighbors who turned out on a chilly

weekday were testimony to that. In an age of bogus, reality show celebrity, Tom Sr.'s acclaim was the genuine article. It seems important, then, to ask how the death of such an ordinary guy could warrant such attention. For, like Willy Loman, who among us doesn't desire the same?

In middle-class, midwestern fashion, Tom Sr.'s life was in most ways unremarkable. He and his wife lived in a modest, beige-brick ranch house with brown shutters. They kept a retiree-issue recreational vehicle parked in the driveway. They wintered at the same Texas campground, and returned home each spring to hunt morel mushrooms at the same spot in northern Michigan. Until his health failed, Tom Sr. drove west each fall with his three sons to hunt pheasants near the same tiny town in North Dakota.

Tom Sr. was a large man, immensely stocky, with a big, open face and a thatch of curly, close-cropped hair. He would have looked good in a Roman toga. His vices were of the fat-cat Republican variety: gas-guzzling cars, big steaks, and well-aged scotch. He had a gruff sense of humor and a likable directness that made him a natural leader. You listened to him with respect, the way you do a good cop or first sergeant.

Tom Sr. could have probably been a state representative had he run for office. Instead, he was called to the thankless, nonpartisan jobs that always need doing in a rural community: township clerk, hospital board member, constable, volunteer fire chief. These were Tom Sr.'s avocation, his civic ministry. He was a forever busy person who spent hundred of hours performing the tedious but necessary duties that most of us claim we're "too busy" to bother with.

I wish I could say that Tom Sr. and I were good friends, but we were not. We knew each other in passing, the way we know the friends of our parents and the parents of our friends. Yet throughout our long acquaintance we did share a rich connection to the same people and rural landscape. And when these bonds are examined you can see why a small town is not only a good place to live but a comforting place to die.

I grew up in Three Rivers and moved to nearby Park Township about forty years later than Tom Sr. did. But our reasons for coming here were similar: affordable homes and real estate, helpful and agreeable neighbors, and plenty of wild places where you can sneak off to hunt or fish whenever the job or kids are making you crazy. There's little commerce apart from a few party stores and a bait shop that operates from a retiree's garage ("Ring Bell *Twice* for Service").

Park Township was named for its parklike groves of burr and white oak, usually no more than twenty-five trees to an acre. The open, grassy terrain was ideal for hunting, and Potawatomi Indians set ground fires to keep the underbrush at bay. Today Tom Sr. lies buried in a nineteenth-century pioneer cemetery that borders his favorite hunting ground. During his last years, even with bad legs and weak lungs, he perched there on an old dining room chair and waited for the deer to come. As much as his headstone, it's this fifteen-acre parcel of woods that enshrines his memory.

The Portage River, which flows about fifty yards south of the cemetery, carries its own current of recollections. For thirty-five years, I've waded these waters in shorts and sneakers to fish for smallmouth bass and pike. A mile downstream is the small woods that I bought from an elderly woman in Detroit, the final remnant of her family's centennial farm. Here, under a century-old beech tree, I proposed to my wife on a windswept December afternoon. To close the circle, I've asked her to scatter my ashes in the river so they can feed the fish. It's the least I can do—I've eaten enough of their kind over the years.

Last things were certainly on the mind of Tom Sr.'s eldest son, Tom Jr., on the morning of his father's funeral. All the boys have followed their father's example of civic service, and for years Tom Jr. has been the Park Township sexton. On summer evenings, you'll often see him at one of the township's four small cemeteries, steering his mower around the gravestones of forgotten pioneers. But there's more to the sexton's job than mowing—he must also make ready the resting place.

When you first realize what Tom Jr.'s job requires of him, the task seems unthinkable. What could be worse than digging your father's grave? But, as it turned out, Tom Jr. didn't have to. His childhood friend Dan, who is also a sexton, dug it for him. (It was only fair since Tom Jr. had earlier dug the grave for Dan's mother.)

If that sounds like a morbid expectation to place on a friendship, think again. Tom Sr.'s grave site is a corner plot bordered by deep woods and pasture. Imagine being out there on a sunny spring morning, alone with your memories and a shovel, doing this most final of chores for a friend's father. How many of us will ever contribute, in such a useful way, to the last remembrance of a loved one?

When the funeral procession reached the cemetery, the sexton's handiwork was hidden beneath a roll of plastic grass. There's no parking lot, so the cars and fire trucks pulled off under a row of walnut trees. On my walk, in I passed the tombstone of another friend's father. This man had taught me to skin squirrels and filet bluegills. He ate snapping turtle meat, hunted raccoons well into his seventies, and told stories about riding the rails as a Depression era hobo.

I also thought of my own seventy-six-year-old father, who'd said his good-byes to Tom Sr. a few weeks earlier. My dad, a Korean War vet, runs a one-man barbershop in Three Rivers. He makes house calls to his bedridden customers and claims that he can smell death. And he smelled it that afternoon when he stopped to give Tom Sr. his final haircut.

While the aura and aroma of death haven't changed, the way we acknowledge it certainly has. Even in conservative midwestern towns, funeral services are billed as Celebrations of Life, complete with Web sites and pop music soundtracks. At a cousin's funeral, "Baba O'Reilly," by the Who, played in the background while friends retold their favorite drinkin' with Dave stories. But at least they spoke from experience. At too many funerals, you'll hear stand-in ministers— summoned from God knows where—who can do little more than mumble vague platitudes about the dead stranger behind them.

At Tom Sr.'s interment, there were no such shenanigans. He was buried as he lived, in proper form. Waiting for us at the cemetery was Father Clark, whose shaved head and black cassock made him resemble a monk more than an Episcopal priest. It was clear that Father Clark did know the deceased. He knew him well, so there was no need for feigned familiarity.

"Thomas was a man of action who didn't believe in folderol," said Father Clark, as we huddled together under a green awning. "Once he knew it was time to die, he set out to get the job done."

The doctors had given Tom Sr. four months to live, but he'd used only a few weeks of this final reprieve. Or perhaps, being an honest man, he needed to repay some of the time he'd borrowed as a Marine Corps rifleman on the hellish beaches of Iwo Jima.

Beneath a weak April sun an American Legion color guard strode forward to provide a last bit of tattered pageantry. They had gimpy legs, potbellies, and hands that fluttered with palsy when they tried to hold a salute. Since childhood, I've known these men as Little League umpires, church ushers, Boy Scout leaders, and idlers at my father's barbershop. Now, in the way of old veterans, their uniforms were no longer uniform but adorned with an eclectic array of ribbons, medals and patriotic trinkets.

For the twenty-one-gun salute, the color guard fired three blank rounds apiece from their well-worn M1 rifles, a weapon Tom Sr. could once field strip blindfolded. Then, with great solemnity, they played "Taps" on a phenomenally scratchy tape player. When a gray legionnaire gave a folded flag to Tom Sr.'s wife, Mary, it wasn't only "from a grateful nation" but from a longtime friend. In this final frail gesture, there was great tribute.

Now only a prayer stood between Tom Sr. and eternity, and with Anglo-Saxon simplicity Father Clark dispensed a powerful blessing. He reached down and grabbed a handful of brown, Michigan loam— the very soil the sexton had dug to honor his friend's father.

"With this," said Father Clark, raising his fist toward heaven, "I commend your soul to God."

Then he scattered the dirt across the polished lid of the coffin. The finality of death, like the conclusion of the ceremony, was unmistakable.

Out of curiosity, I watched to see if the genteel Father Clark would wipe his hand after his dramatic graveside display. He did not, and after the ceremony sandy smudges remained on his leatherbound Book of Common Prayer.

UNDERSTANDING WINTER

From the backdoor of my farmhouse, the morning sun creeps above the frosted beige carpet of a soybean field. For a moment, it oozes like a globe of orange jelly between the oaks that stand in silhouette against the field's eastern boundary. Then, freed from the horizon's grasp, it illumines a ribbon of high clouds in regal shades of gold and tangerine.

It's a fleeting and glorious picture, but you'd never know it by listening to the local radio station. The meteorologist, from his soundproofed studio in a city twenty-five miles away, can only warn of the minus-one-degree wind chill. "It's a ter-r-r-ibly cold morning," he says, a sentiment echoed by his fellow disc jockey.

But cold compared to what? This is Michigan, and it's January, so the weather is hardly abnormal. There's been no snowstorm to impede traffic or interrupt electrical service. And the Chicken Little broadcasters, along with the vast majority of their audience, are cosseted within a building or vehicle where the temperature rarely dips below sixty-five degrees.

It makes me wonder what the presettlement Great Lakes Indians would have thought of us. They had good reason to be afraid of the cold. They slept in bark-walled lodges atop mats of woven reeds and deerskin. Their stores of dried berries, wild rice, and venison had to last until the spring maple-sugaring season. In lean years, they feared the Windigo, a man-eating spirit that stalked the winter woods looking for humans to devour.

By comparison, there's no rational reason why healthy, modern Americans should fear winter's hardships. In the past fifty years, we have nearly engineered cold weather discomfort out of existence. We live in centrally heated houses with attached, semiheated garages. Our cars and sport-utility vehicles, which can be started from indoors by remote control, come with heated steering wheels, heated seats, and heated side mirrors. For personal insulation, we can buy—at bargain prices—coats, boots, hats, and gloves that are wonderfully warm, lightweight, and waterproof. After fifty thousand years, the human race has come in from the cold in a big way.

By all accounts, our technology has pounded a Teflon stake into winter's icy heart. So why should we fear and even demonize everyday winter weather?

Perhaps it's because we no longer understand winter's practical and spiritual purpose. Living as we do, it's hard to appreciate the season's age-old function as a time of rest and reflection woven into the cycle of seasons.

That traditional perception of winter is summed up beautifully by the folksinger Jean Ritchie in the hymn "Winter Grace." Ritchie isn't daunted or depressed by the cold, quiet months she spends on her Kentucky farm. Rather, she seems to profit by them. She sings of winter as "a time for man and beast to stand and watch the seasons turn, to watch the stars for secret signs and God's true lessons learned."

There are still thousands of square miles in rural America where people can find winter's stillness. Yet farmers comprise only 2 percent of the population, and even most country dwellers earn their daily bread "in town." And in cities and suburbs forever lit by the orange pall of sodium lights it's hard to attune our senses to the season's subtle signals. To complicate matters, our daily perceptions of winter are contorted by the mass media. Under the guise of keeping us well informed, the media's weather coverage often makes us unduly alarmed.

In the 1970s, when my family's TV set received only three VHF channels, the weather report came last on the 6:00 p.m. and 11:00 p.m. newscast. My favorite weatherman was a portly, bald-headed fellow from South Bend, Indiana. He wore a mustard yellow sport coat and slapped magnetic suns and snow clouds on a U.S. map as he delivered his forecasts. He warned viewers if a big storm was coming, but he never got hysterical about it. In fact, I don't recall that he ever used the term *lake-effect snow event*. A winter snowstorm, much like dead alewives on the beach in springtime, was something to expect when you lived near the Lake Michigan shore.

The tone and scope of weather coverage changed after the Weather Channel was introduced in 1982. Its success (the network reached eighty-five million households by 2003) proved that weather news was an untapped source of high drama and ratings. Following the Weather Channel's lead, TV stations began to cover weather as a fast-breaking news story. Improved digital and satellite technology, along with affordable live-broadcast equipment, allowed local stations to present weather news in a more detailed and breathless fashion.

These days, even when a mundane snowstorm drops two inches, a weather story will lead the local newscast. Meteorologists gleefully announce windchill indexes and proclaim "weather advisories" for every imaginable variety of ice, rain, wind, fog, or snow. From an early age, we are now taught to fear winter weather the way we're supposed to fear strangers and bad cholesterol.

During rare bouts of extreme weather, improved coverage can help save lives. But most of the time, at least in southern Michigan, it's simply overkill. How many times, for instance, have you seen this bit of newsroom theater? There's been a snow "event" predicted, but nothing has fallen yet except a few flurries. Nonetheless, the news anchor will cut to a live shot of some young, red-nosed reporter shivering in light snow by the interstate. It's as if we needed the imprimatur of TV to confirm what we can see from our own front door: that only a few flakes are indeed falling from the sky.

Another flawed way in which television encourages us to experience winter is as a marketing prop. Forget the debate over whether the holidays and Christmas trees are of Christian, druid, or Wall Street origin. Winter's entire persona has been co-opted by the marketplace. However, instead of making us fear winter the marketers want us to buy it: the industrial-strength consumerism of Santa Claus, Inc.; the L. L. Bean fantasies of polar-fleece-clad families skiing and spending their way through clapboard villages in the azure

New England dusk; and even the dancing dollars that pimp Lincoln and Washington during appliance store ads for Presidents' Day sales. From early November to mid-February, the commerce gods wrap their appeals in archetypal winter images. They evoke in us a vague sense of longing that we can't quite identify or satisfy.

That's why it's good to remember that winter's true fruits are free for the taking. There may be a good example of that right outside your window. In nature, creatures instinctively sense that winter is a time for stillness and interior growth. This is true not just for animals but for less sentient beings such as well.

After the gaudy exuberance of autumn, after their fiery leaves have withered and blown away, deciduous trees direct their life force inward. It may look like they have nothing to do but wait for spring. But to prepare for frigid weather many trees and woody plants undergo a process known as hardening off. The sap withdraws from their twigs and branches and returns to the roots. The roots may continue to grow until the ground freezes solid. This growth, though hidden from view, will nurture the tree and everything that shares its benefits. Winter's hiatus makes possible the amber delight of maple syrup and the green canopy of shade on a hot August day.

Despite the inevitable distractions of a 24–7 culture, I suspect that many of us would like our winters to be more rewarding as well. We are not like those hysterical disc jockeys who quiver at the sight of a wayward icicle. We would welcome winter pursuits that enrich the mind, body and soul. But, alas, our everyday reality requires otherwise. In the heart of winter, it is dark when we leave for work and dark when we return. And, if you're like me, your job involves no contact with nature aside from a short walk from the parking garage to the office (connected by a glass tube that coworkers have fittingly dubbed the Hamster Tunnel).

So during the week one has to improvise. I am lucky in that most of my forty-five-minute commute takes me along a two-lane highway through farm country. And it's here that I've found winter solace in a most unnatural way: while sitting on my rear end and contemplating creation through a dirty windshield.

The desired mental state I'm after is similar to *lectio divinia*, the ancient practice of inspired scriptural reading. With *lectio divinia*, the idea is to read slowly and stop and reflect when you feel drawn to a certain passage. What I try to achieve on the road is a mobile meditation, a *lectio divinia* of the landscape.

The all-important first step is to turn off the radio. Then, as much as safe driving allows, open your mind to the passing countryside until a particular scene evokes a heightened sense of peace and beauty. Of course, it's not as easy as it sounds, especially when you've driven the same route for ten years. Nor is it always possible to free your jabbering mind from office politics or the nagging details of a home renovation project. On the other hand, *lectio divinia* probably isn't easy for monks who have spent twenty-five years rereading the same Bible. But, contrary to what Ecclesiastes claimed, there is always something new to see under the sun.

Perhaps the crimson sunrise will summon up a forgotten hymn or memory from childhood. Or maybe shadows in the snow will appear indigo blue, the color my grandma loved to use in her winter landscape oil paintings. On foggy mornings, when hoarfrost brings a furry roundness to each branch and twig, a single tree in a cornfield may shine like a burning bush, backlit by the low-angled sun. Such scenes are lovely but ephemeral. Ten seconds later the conditions that produced them are gone forever and the miraculous fades into the ordinary. As Robert Frost once wrote of happiness, these encounters make up in height what they lack in length.

On weekends, though, it's possible to encounter winter on more intimate terms. There's wood to split and haul for the fireplace, and we have two kids and a tireless dog that always need outdoor exercise. For longer outings, there's a nature preserve down the road where it's quiet enough to hear the oak leaves rattle like castanets in the north wind.

In southern Michigan, early winter also provides some of the best weather for outdoor labor. The weekends between Thanksgiving and Christmas, before frost tightens the soil, are usually a good time to transplant trees. A few years ago, in early December, I recall a Saturday afternoon perfectly suited for such work. With temperatures in the low forties, it was warm enough to dig in a flannel shirt and army fatigue pants. Then, suddenly, as I packed topsoil around the dormant roots of a hackberry tree, it was as if I felt the seasons turn.

It was a windless, monochrome day with no shadows with which to measure the passing hours. The only signs of life were the delicate buds that swelled from the springy tips of shiny branches. The sap may have fled to the roots, but the buds had their own story to tell. On close inspection, you could see the promise of next year's growth, the leaves and flowers condensed into tiny, spheroid bundles. At the appointed time, these buds will open. Until then, like a tired boxer waiting out the long count, they'll use the respite of winter to their full advantage.

In the course of informal research (i.e., snooping around), I've found a few old masters who still spend their winters in a similar fashion. In other words, out of choice or necessity, they've conformed to the hardships and rewards that winter has to offer. As you might expect, these are folks who neither commute nor compute. Yet there's much we can learn from them, even if we wouldn't want to live exactly as they do.

My wife's Uncle Dayton runs a seven-hundred-acre fruit and vegetable farm in Southwest Michigan. During the growing season, his workdays may stretch from sunrise to 10:00 p.m. and his weeks know no weekends. In winter, Dayton mainly prunes grapes and maintains his farm equipment. The shorter, less hectic days give him time to labor in other vineyards as well. So in his bib overalls, with size-fifteen feet propped near an old woodstove, Dayton commits himself to literary self-improvement. Not just nursery catalogs or the *Wall Street Journal* but the classics. One year he read the collected works of Shakespeare during his winter sabbatical.

To me, Dayton's winter schedule provides an ideal balance of reflection and quiet, useful labor. Picture him in the February solitude of an orchard, his hands busy, his mind pleasantly occupied with the play or sonnet he read the night before. The tending of vines and fruit trees—tasks as old as civilization—must give him a great perspective on the timeless themes of Shakespeare.

You have to admire Dayton's intellectual discipline. By means of imitation, I've vowed to finish two of Thomas Merton's books on contemplation before the ice breaks up on the St. Joseph River. Because, if not in winter, when? Winter is meant for hearty fare. It's a time to savor not only my wife's homemade chicken and spaghetti squash soup but to read those serious tomes that have languished at the bedside since the fish started biting last spring. There's also time, after kids' baths and stories, for the fireside talks that help two adults remember why they live together.

The importance of that was reinforced in a picturesque way one February evening when my brother and I visited an Amish farmer near Centreville. We wanted the farmer to repair the old windmill that my brother uses to irrigate his parking-lot-sized vegetable garden. It was near dusk, and we found the family milking cows by hand in the basement of their whitewashed barn. As she worked, a teenaged girl in a black bonnet sang a German hymn, sweet and clear in the crisp air. Mom, Grandpa and several kids were there, talking and laughing in the pale glow of a kerosene lantern.

In summer, milking might have fallen to one or more of the children. In winter, with less to do around the farm, it was a family chore. They milked steadily but not hastily. The slower pace of winter had drawn tight the Amish bonds of social and economic togetherness.

Heading home, we passed a black-shuttered ranch house edged by yew bushes. The contrast between this somnolent place and the Amish farm couldn't have been more clear. Through a big picture window I could see a family inside this home, too. They sat on couches and easy chairs but didn't face each other. The object of their attention cast a ghostly blue glow, which flickered across faces that appeared vacant.

I've certainly spent my share of winter nights sitting lethargic and slack jawed in front of a TV set. And it's true that a northern winter is the most trying of seasons. The sun may not shine for weeks on end, and the night wind howls at the door like a hungry wolf. Nevertheless, we can choose to dispel this outer bleakness with timeless pleasures such as good books, good conversation, and the soul-sustaining meals that no one has time for in summer. For the frozen solitude of winter is not a thing to be feared. Winter is simply an old friend returned who waits in unspoken silence to wish us well.

WHAT'S RIGHT ABOUT
THE NIGHT

One of the things I love most about living in the country is the darkness of the night sky. There's never been a yard light outside our farmhouse. We haven't wanted man-made illumination to interfere with the panorama of stars and planets overhead. To gaze into the eternal depths until your neck gets stiff helps put your trifling troubles and desires into the proper perspective.

The velvety cloak of night also brings a welcome sense of closure to the day. For me, the ritual of putting animals to bed in a barn (even if it's just a dog and cat) feels more complete when you can leave a darkened building and field behind you.

Nonetheless, darkness can also hide a multitude of sins, which is why our urbanized world equates bright lights with safety. This can hold true for country dwellers as well. We discovered that on the frigid January night when our barn was intentionally set on fire. Whoever did the deed was never caught. Some say the arsonist may have been emboldened by the patch of darkness that surrounds our property. Whatever the motive, the horrific sight of this timber-frame landmark engulfed in flames is a memory that will never leave me.

Our new wooden barn is all we could want; an Amish work crew and a generous insurance check have seen to that. But, like the old one, it has no external lights—and that poses a dilemma. On one hand, I'd like to keep this barn secure, and a yard light of Death Star magnitude would supposedly deter mischief. Yet I am unwilling to sacrifice my starry sky to the tyranny of a petty criminal.

If we think of darkness at all, we tend to view it as simply an absence of light. It's an inky void that cries out to be filled with some form of man-made illumination. What we've forgotten, in this over-electrified age, is that darkness itself is a valuable resource. And that it serves an important purpose for many living creatures.

We in fact have an inborn need for darkness. For humans, too much light during sleeping hours can cause depression, grogginess, and impaired thinking. Scientists from the Centers for Disease Control theorize that sleeping in a room that's bathed by the glow of a streetlight can contribute to hormone-related cancers. A University of Pennsylvania study found that children younger than age two who slept with a nightlight on were more likely to develop nearsightedness before they reached adulthood.

For animals, too much artificial light can be lethal. Birds, which navigate by the stars and moon, are easily confused by bright lights. They die by the thousands each year as they crash into buildings and radio towers. Wild salmon fry prefer to swim at night through deep, dark water in streams and rivers. When artificial lights lure them to the shallows, they become easy prey for predators. Young sea turtles, after they hatch from nests along the beach, are often fatally attracted to streetlights and floodlit parking lots.

Light pollution is far worse today than it was a few decades ago. On average, a modern, single-family home uses 40 percent more kilowatt-hours of lighting than in 1970. Much of this costly illumination never even hits its intended target. Experts estimate that up to one-third of all outdoor lighting is misdirected. It shines upward and sideways and does little more than bathe the sky in a wasteful display of electricity.

For the outside of our new barn, an electrician friend suggested that we install gooseneck fixtures with circular shields to aim the light downward—the kind used by gas stations during the 1940s and 1950s. He also recommended motion detectors, which will activate the lights only when there's an intruder present.

The new barn is five years old, but we've yet to install any of these precautionary devices. Call it laziness or a false sense of security, but exterior lights really haven't been necessary. Most of us can rise groggy from sleep and make our way, without incident, from a dark bed to the bathroom. It's no different with a dark barn. Once you know the way, it's easy enough to navigate around the flowerpots and firewood. And with snow on the ground it's almost bright enough outside on a winter night to read a newspaper.

Then it could be that our quaintly unlit barn is just asking for it. A few weeks ago, an arsonist struck again, this time torching a dilapidated old barn just outside the Three Rivers city limits. It looked like the same modus operandi to me. "Sparky" picked another building with bone-dry, weathered siding that would go up like a propane torch.

Perhaps I should be afraid of a follow-up visit, but I'm not. More than anything, what I feel for him is pity. All you can do is say a little prayer for his tortured soul and hope that he'll someday be caught and have his head examined. Otherwise, Sparky's final destination may give him more flames than he bargained for.

I'll probably never understand why someone would burn down a beautiful old barn. I don't think I want to. But I do know that what we see in the evening sky—whether it's the diamond twinkle of stars or the orange glare of suburbia—is a reflection of how we view the world. And we shouldn't allow the darkness that lies within a few human hearts to overcome what's good about the night.

IT'S TRUE—YOU MAY
ALREADY BE A WINNER

Sometime each February, millions of Americans receive an oversized envelope proclaiming that they "may already be a winner." Statistically, there's a tiny chance that Ed McMahon (or whoever the sweepstakes shill may be) is telling the truth. Maybe the Prize Patrol will pull into our driveway, and maybe cashing a surfboard-sized check with six zeroes will bring us endless happiness.

As with most pipe dreams, this one always seemed harmless enough. But that changed after I had a disturbing premonition about the way abundant wealth might affect my life. It was an experience much like the scene from *A Christmas Carol* when the ghost of Christmas yet to come gives Scrooge the biggest scare of all.

My encounter took place in rural Michigan, where I'd been asked to help sort through a lifetime collection of books and furnishings. It was the lonely cargo of a retirement dream home: the husband was dead, his ailing widow had been hospitalized, and there were no children.

I didn't know the couple, but as we worked through the clutter a picture of their lives began to emerge. They were clearly well-educated with refined tastes and expansive intellects. They left hundreds of good books on music, psychology, nature, ethnic folklore, herbal medicine, and organic gardening. Their arts and crafts furniture was elegantly sturdy and harmonized nicely with the cedar paneling and woodstove ambience of the house.

The couple had retired to the country in the late 1970s, pursuing a cultivated passion for back to nature living. In their private Eden they planted an orchard of fruit trees, a grove of chestnuts, and a tidy and respectable garden. They raised their own chickens and ate organic beef. There was a filing cabinet full of lively correspondence from nurseries and specialty farms across the country.

The trajectory of their lives both troubled and intrigued me. Like them, I live in the country and am eager to create a hobby farmer's nirvana. Like them, I love the books and philosophy of rural life almost as much as its substance. The main difference, however, is that this couple had enough money to make their dreams a reality.

But eventually, as it must for us all, their time ran out. On the day of my visit, their once lovely country estate was filthy and forlorn. Dead mice littered the bathroom tub, and stray cats had soiled the hardwood floors and countertops. Everything in the unheated house reeked of cobwebs, mildew, and despair.

The real pathos of the place didn't register at first. The manager of the upcoming estate sale was there with her crew, and we all hovered about the house like vultures over a carcass. (Not unlike the cockney washerwoman who brashly sorted through Scrooge's curtains and bedclothes during the apparition of his death.)

As for me, my mother buys and sells used books, and I was there to help her cart away the heavy boxes. An hour or so later, after everyone else had left, the morose setting prompted some deeper reflection. What had happened here? Aside from succumbing to the usual perils of sickness and old age, how had the dream of this well-meaning couple fared so badly?

In the basement was the first indication that something, or some-one, had gone haywire. First I saw thousands of moldering magazines and newspapers, all bound with twine and long since forgotten. There were hundreds of planting pots and plastic tubs and heaps of unused garden tools, many still in their packages. Even for someone who loves gardening, it was an embarrassment—or more accurately a pathology—of riches. There was enough here to equip a small commercial greenhouse. It had all been hoarded beyond reason, more than any two people could ever use or care for. Now the sad harvest of their miserly eccentricity was a pile of rubbish big enough to fill a twenty-foot Dumpster. Their pastoral paradise had come to this.

So, again, what had happened here?

Without personal details, one can only make generalizations based on the cursory evidence. Given the bizarre quantity of near-useless possessions, it's likely that mental imbalance was a factor. Yet before things reached that point the couple may have fallen prey to an affliction that nearly every middle-class American struggles with.

One night while they were sleeping, perhaps, the snake of materialism snuck into the garden. It wasn't an ugly snake. In the way of mythical serpents, it may have come disguised as something good or alluring. Maybe something you'd see in the stylish pages of a Plow and Hearth or Smith and Hawken catalog.

From that point on, simplicity became more complicated and happiness became predicated on acquisition rather than subsistence. Gradually, trips to the garden store, and lounging on the sofa with garden catalogs, seemed more fun than weeding the garden. That old rusty rake? We need two new ones with rubber handgrips and shiny green tines. The weathered hoes we left leaning against the garage all winter? Here's a new Swedish model with an orthopedic handle that's hewn from European ash. And for the kitchen how about this gorgeous, hammered-copper compost pail?

But here's the sad part: once home from the store, or unwrapped from its FedEx package, the new tool or designer doodad often loses much of its appeal. It may seem small, dull, or inconsequential. As with most impulse purchases, it was the buying, not the having, that brought the most pleasure.

If this story sounds familiar, it should. American-style consumerism is one of the most potent and adaptive social forces in human history. It transcends all boundaries of geography, religion, and culture. It creeps into everything we do, and more than we know it shapes our world and determines what we care about. From the earliest age, we program our children to desire and acquire ("collecting" we call it). There's no hiding from the beast of consumerism even if you flee to a quiet place in the country. It will lurk in the garden, and certainly in your mailbox, ever eager for the chance to consume *you.*

For instance, on the occasion of my daughter's birth, I planted an apple tree. A nice gesture, most people would agree. But here's where consumerism, disguised as a country squire, raised its avaricious head. Once the apple tree was in the ground, it was like I'd caught a case of mental poison ivy. Buying that tree had scratched an itch, and all I wanted was to scratch it some more—with a wallet-sized piece of plastic, of course.

For days afterward, my mind raced with plans to buy more fruit trees, as well as blueberry bushes, livestock fences, grapevines, a new tool shed. This greedy obsession threatened to turn a healthy interest into a joyless, anxious craving.

The fever passed, but the virus lingers on. Given a blank check, I could easily buy enough rural simplicity to overcomplicate my life and alienate me from everyone I hold dear. It's a problem that I once heard a Franciscan nun describe this way: "Some people are like little children with their mouths full of candy. Instead of tasting what they have, they only want to cram in more."

Henry David Thoreau, the patron saint of thrift, offered this advice: "Beware of all enterprises that require new clothes and not rather a new wearer of clothes. . . . If you have any enterprise before you, try it in your old clothes."

In other words, appreciate your customized garden gloves—the pair with a thumb chewed half off by a naughty puppy. Keep for summer wear the old boots, now curled at the toes and speckled with barn paint, which helped you hike the Lake Superior shore. Apply deck sealer to the wooden handles of your garden rakes so that they'll last twenty years or so (unless you decapitate one with a riding mower like I did last summer).

Over time, if we resist the itch of consumerism, we'll find that Ed McMahon and the Prize Patrol are right: most of us are winners already. May the treasures we have at hand—in a world so filled with real need—always be enough.

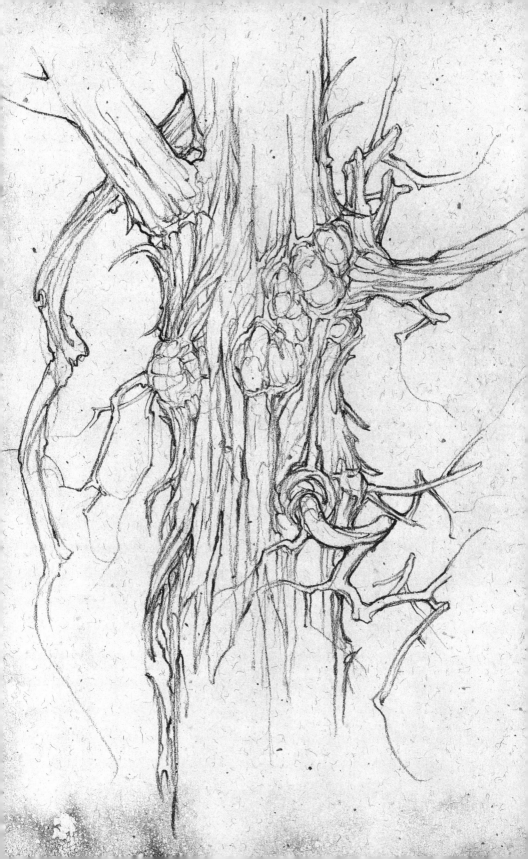

Text design by Mary H. Sexton

Typesetting by Delmastype, Ann Arbor, Michigan

Text Font: Perpetua

Perpetua, type designer Eric Gill's most popular Roman typeface, was
released by the Monotype Corporation between 1925 AND 1932. It first
appeared in a limited edition of the book *The Passion of Perpetua and Felicity,*
for which the typeface was named. The italic form was originally called
Felicity. Perpetua's clean chiseled look recalls Gill's stonecutting work
and makes it an excellent text typeface, giving sparkle to long passages
of text; the Perpetua capitals have beautiful, classical lines that make this
one of the finest display alphabets available.

—courtesy adobe.com